STEP-PARENTING

A practical guide for everyone facing
this increasingly common situation

In the same series
ADDICTIONS
AGORAPHOBIA
BRINGING UP A MENTALLY HANDICAPPED CHILD
COPING WITH CANCER
COT DEATHS
DEAFNESS IN THE ADULT
DEPRESSION
DIVORCE
EPILEPSY
I CAN'T FACE TOMORROW
LIVING WITH A COLOSTOMY
OVERCOMING DISFIGUREMENT
REDUNDANCY
SCHIZOPHRENIA

STEP-PARENTING

Understanding the emotional problems and stresses

Christine Atkinson

THORSONS PUBLISHING GROUP
Wellingborough, Northamptonshire
Rochester, Vermont

First published June 1986
Second Impression October 1986

© CHRISTINE ATKINSON 1986

All rights reserved. No part of this book may be reproduced or utilized in any form or by any means, electronic or mechanical, including photocopying, recording or by any information storage and retrieval system, without permission in writing from the Publisher.

> British Library Cataloguing in Publication Data
>
> Atkinson, Christine
>   Step-parenting: understanding the emotional problems and stresses.
>   1. Step-children — Family relationships
>   2. Parent and child   3. Step-parents
>   I. Title
>   306.8'74   HQ777.7
>
> ISBN 0-7225-1264-3

Printed and bound in Great Britain

CONTENTS

		Page
	Introduction	7
Chapter		
1.	Planning: Preliminaries	11
2.	Planning: Practicalities	29
3.	The Interim Period	45
4.	Loyalties and Jealousies	53
5.	Parent, Ex-Parent and Step-Parent	65
6.	Relatives and Friends	77
7.	Togetherness	83
8.	Joys	89
9.	Have I Got What It Takes?	95
10.	Help!	101
	Conclusion	105
	Further Information	107
	Index	109

This book is dedicated to Michael, Christopher and Robin, without whom I would not be a step-parent!

INTRODUCTION

I have written this book out of a desire to help prospective step-parents to look ahead at the coming years and try to foresee what kind of difficulties might be in store for them. If this sounds ridiculous — after all, who wants to know about hard times until they actually come — think again. As a prospective step-parent you are about to join a family unit consisting of one or more children and a parent. You might compare the situation to that of a skin graft. You are the patch, taken from elsewhere, which hopefully will blend in with the surrounding area and eventually become indistinguishable from the original piece. We all know that it takes a long time for a skin graft to 'take' but do we also appreciate that it will take quite some time before the step-family situation becomes indistinguishable from the normal one? A skin graft is a delicate operation and must be skilfully handled. I believe that a step-marriage is also a delicate operation in its early stages and that all too often we go ahead without the due consideration that is demanded.

When getting married under normal circumstances you can get to know your partner very well in your own time. There are no children — these come when you want them to. In a step-marriage, one or maybe both of you will have another person's child or children to bring up. The children will have characteristics you couldn't possibly have known or guessed beforehand, even if you do try to get to know them closely before you marry into the family. As they grow older each stage of growth will bring its own problems and surprises and although this is so in any marriage with children, in your particular case there is no natural bond between you and your step-children; they do not feel obliged by nature to do as you ask, or behave as you would wish them to. They might feel resentments which to you seem utterly unfair, but how do you really know what they feel about their real parents? Even a baby step-child will perceive a difference between the way you hold him and the way his own parent did. When you deal with your own child's behaviour you recognize in him a few traits from you and your partner, with possibly some from grandparents also. In the case of your step-child, half of him is unknown to you, (presuming that you did not know the other parent well). When we see our own characteristics reflected in our children, we can usually put ourselves in their position and act accordingly, with understanding, but handling an unknown quantity is quite another thing. You could compare it to a teacher trying to handle a difficult child at school, not knowing anything at all about his or her background and upbringing.

You will see by now what I am driving at. You cannot deceive yourself into thinking that this marriage is not all that different from any other. It is, to begin with at least, and once you have accepted this fact you are likely to have a better chance of making it a success. However, lest you be faltering already, this is a book of encouragement and is meant as a practical help and guide. What I ask you to do first of all is to take your time over the decision to take on another person's family. The family unit is all-important in our society and this particular family expects you to be one of its two mainstays. The step-marriage is a very responsible undertaking. Sit quietly with your partner and go through the parts of this guide relevant to your own situation, make your decisions together, and reach working compromises where complete agreement is impossible. Involve the children too if their ages and natures allow it but tread carefully here; they will need very sensitive handling.

You may find that certain areas of the guide do not apply to you. This is more than likely since very few cases can be identical in view of the human element involved so ignore these parts. After all, this can only be a general guide to a very complex subject.

The chapter on planning is all-important in my opinion. Too many second marriages have quickly foundered because the partners involved thought they already knew the ropes and would be sure to succeed second time round. With an 'instant' family as well as a new partner to cope with, do not hope for immediate success. Remember the skin graft and be patient, and when the bad moments seem to be outnumbering the good, just remember that this is often how a 'normal' family exists; everyone has their ups and downs, arguments and crises.

Although the book is meant primarily for those embarking on step-parenthood, I am sure that those of you who are already involved can benefit greatly. If you feel that you are at the end of your tether, totally inadequate for the job, and ready to give up in the face of too many difficulties, then I would advise you to turn straight away to Chapter 10. Perhaps you feel the need for this chapter first even though you have not yet married into your 'family'. There are limits to one person's abilities under certain circumstances and it is a sign of strength rather than weakness to ask for help.

In order to present a balanced picture of the step-family and its inherent problems, it is essential to represent the views of the step-children themselves as well as those of their parents. There are indeed two sides to every coin. Remember that *you* chose to marry; in most cases the children involved had no choice in the matter. Once you understand how *they* might be feeling, you will have a better foundation for building up your family relationships. They may not be able to tell you how they are feeling either because you are (as yet) unapproachable or because they cannot put it all into words. At the end of many chapters I have added case histories and quotations from children I talked to in preparing this material. Their ages ranged from fifteen to forty — the term 'children' is used literally — and they spoke to me in private but with parental consent where necessary. In many cases the children experienced pain whilst looking back to the bereavement period after a death or divorce, but each was certain that if their account was going to help any other step-family members to have an easier time, it was well worth 'digging deep'.

I was most impressed by their lucidity and accuracy in expressing feelings which most of us would find hard to put into words, and particularly touched to find a distinct lack of animosity among them. They were nearly all pleased about the marriage for their parent's sake but many mentioned that the choice was not theirs. Their main grievances, I think, can be summed up in a nutshell — they felt that *their* feelings at the time of changing the family structure had not been considered sufficiently — and this is something all potential step-parents should bear in mind.

A final point I would like to make at this stage is by no means the least important. Many people feel odd, different or alone against the rest of the world when they anticipate a marriage which is not exactly straightforward. How wrong can they be! Official statistics concerning second marriages, step-marriages, one parent families, etc. are absolutely astounding! I did hear a young girl the other day say to her mother, 'You know, Mum, we feel quite out of it in our class. Nearly all the others have interesting backgrounds with new parents, step-relations and so on, we're only normal and boring, aren't we?' Need I say more? A survey by our local headmaster in his very typical school revealed that over a third of the pupils had these 'interesting' backgrounds. So you are most definitely not alone or different or bad or whatever other word you have found for yourself; you are simply human and a product of our times. Please take heart and read on, and remember, by no means all of the problems discussed will be yours but you might meet up with some of them, however, as the grafting process takes place.

1.

PLANNING: PRELIMINARIES

I think, with hindsight, that my own step-family unit is very fortunate to have worked out reasonably well, since we did not sit down and plan it all out beforehand. However, now that I can look back on thirteen years' experience of step-parenting and have also done much research into the subject by talking to many other step-parents and children, I can confidently relay this message: get together with your partner and really thrash out all the pros and cons you can envisage connected with your particular version of step-parenting. I say 'your particular version' because no two situations and backgrounds can be the same; yours is unique. However, it does fit into a general pattern and we must talk in terms of that pattern in order to simplify matters.

Previously, you might not have given much thought to the subject of step-parenting, since it has never been particularly well publicized, but now that you are contemplating it, the enormity of the move you are about to make will strike you. 'How will I perform as a mother/father?' wonders the first-time-married step-parent (my own chief worry in those days). 'What if they hate me the minute they set eyes on me?'; 'What if my children and his/hers don't get on?'; 'Will I be able to cope without those first blissful years alone with my partner?'; 'When will I ever get a moment to myself from now on?'; 'I bet the neighbours will gossip when they see that I'm too young to have all this lot round me.' These and a hundred and one other questions will be buzzing around your head by the time you sit down to plan things out with your partner.

Don't panic. Remember two important facts. First, there are two of you to cope; your future partner loves you and will be at your side as helper and go-between. Secondly, there are simply thousands of other folk in similar situations to yours who are learning to cope and thousands more who have survived all the initial fears, doubts and hurdles. There is safety in numbers!

A cut and dried recipe for success can never be found, in view of the many different variations on the theme of step-parenting and the essentially human elements involved, but here are a few guidelines which I hope will help to focus your attention on the problems in general and lead you on to consider those more relevant to you in particular. They are not necessarily in any order of importance.

Do You Both Agree on the Basic Principles of Bringing Up Children?

If you find you clash loudly on certain aspects of upbringing, it is far better to discover the fact now when there is still time to do something about it, rather than make some awful discovery later which catches you both on the hop. You can probably agree on a working compromise if you find it impossible to reach perfect agreement, which will ensure that you present a united front when situations arise. There is nothing worse than a child seeing two different sets of standards, one for mum and one for dad. He will quickly learn to play the one parent off against the other and could grow up in great confusion and insecurity, unsure of which set of standards to follow. A child likes to know where he stands even if he doesn't care for certain disagreeable rules and regulations, for it gives him a sense of stability and continuity which, in the case of a remarriage, is all important to him since he has probably already suffered during the previous period of bereavement or divorce.

Here are a few questions to ask yourselves:

Bedtimes: Do you have views about a certain time for a certain age-group?
Television: Do you mind what type of programmes the children view or how much time they spend in front of a television?
Responsibilities: Do you believe in sharing out the family jobs

Schooling: in order to give a sense of responsibility to the children, for example, walking the dog, cleaning the car, taking on a small section of garden? This is an important question, having a great bearing on the child's future and happiness. Talk about your ideals with respect to schooling, visit the local schools if you are moving to a new area. What are your views on homework? Will you try to go to school events together?

Privacy: Will you organize a room where the children can be away from you both if they feel the need to be on their own at times?

Punishment: Are you both agreed on the basic principles of crime and punishment? This sounds terribly Victorian but is nevertheless an important subject for you to discuss, since it is necessary for your children to know what to expect if they commit any of the common crimes of childhood. For example, do you both consider lying to be a punishable offence and if it became regular how would you stop it? Remember that a united front is very important even if it means compromising your separate opinions.

These are all questions that 'normal' parents have to face too, but the big difference is that they can deal with everything from scratch as it occurs — you two cannot do this. One of you (or even both in the double step-marriage) is a newcomer to the 'small fry' of the family. You have your own ideas on how to be a good parent and what to expect of children, but these particular children have been brought up to live by certain standards over which you had no control. The real question, therefore, is whether you as the newcomer can accept the status quo happily, or whether you feel strongly that there ought to be a few changes. More will be said about this later but in the meantime a united front as joint parents is the thing to aim for.

Many other questions must spring into mind when you think of your future step-children and their endearing (or otherwise) characteristics, to say nothing of the different natures of your partner and yourself. Many an awkward future situation could well be averted now by a bit of honest self-questioning and at the same time you will be getting to know more and more about your partner-to-be and his or her children. This leads us on nicely to the next question:

How Well Do You Know Your Future Family?
Do you feel you know them well enough to become their mum or dad? This is a big question and if the answer is a definite 'no', now is the time to start getting to know them, before marriage rather than after. Common ground is what you need to establish first — something that you and the children can both relate to without conscious effort. Being a natural tomboy I was off to a good start with my three boisterous boys — we could climb the same tree, scramble across the same rocky ridge, have camping expeditions and endless arm-wrestling matches (I soon lost out at these!). I admit that I was lucky and our common interests probably helped us a lot through our 'acquaintanceship' period. Look hard for your own common ground, and make your first move upon it. It might only be something insignificant or trivial such as a mutual passion for ice-cream but if you and the children share this passion it will be a bond between you, however small, from which bigger things can grow.

Children are quick to spot things you never dreamed they were 'mature' or 'aware' enough to notice. You will probably find that they will blow all your carefully-laid plans to meet casually and be 'friends' by chirping up with such comments as 'When is Daddy going to marry you?' or 'When you are my mum I'm going to pretend you're my real one'. Never underestimate children, particularly in delicate personal situations. Having said that, I still think it is worthwhile 'engineering' some casual meetings, using ground familiar to the children so that you can get the feel of each other without making deliberate and conscious efforts to establish a parent-child relationship.

Casual Meetings
A visit to the cinema is an ideal way in which to get together with the future family without feeling that awful sensation at the pit of the stomach as you wonder, 'What if he hates me?' or 'What

if I go and put my foot in it before we've even had the chance to get to know each other?' I'm sure all prospective step-parents get these qualms and fears before their first meetings with the dreaded step-children (I certainly did), so it is worth working out the best way for you to get over this first hurdle. Try not to build up any pictures in your mind about how it will be; concentrate on being your ordinary natural self otherwise you might risk giving a totally false impression to the children. If you are a jeans and sweater fanatic, for instance, it's not a good idea to get dressed up to the nines in frills and stilettos for your first meeting. For one thing you will feel ill at ease and a stranger to yourself, let alone them; and for another the children will not know which is the real you. Just pretend that the children belong to a friend who has asked you to look after them for an hour or so. Not easy advice I know, but it might help to calm your nerves and enable you to behave naturally. The cinema idea is particularly good because you are sitting in the dark (thus hiding your fears!) and can laugh or be frightened at the same things, which creates some sort of bond between you.

During these occasional meetings and outings the children can view you simply as a friend of their mum or dad rather than as a threatening figure straight from a fairy tale, the wicked step-mother or step-father. They can either like or dislike you for reasons grounded on facts rather than those influenced and distorted by dark imaginings. Gradually a relationship will build up through sheer familiarity until you are ready for the next step in the procedure, the introduction of the idea of marriage.

During my discussions with other step-children two particularly relevant examples arose regarding this introductory period of getting to know one another.

Susan and her sister
At the age of twelve, with a sister aged ten, Susan was suddenly confronted with a shower of little presents and gifts of sweets from the gentleman her divorced mother was friendly with. She was more astute than her little sister and immediately saw this as a bribe to gain affection. She instantly resented this procedure knowing it wasn't genuine affection at all and developed a hearty dislike for the man who subsequently became her step-father. The marriage was immediately off to a bad start and has never

been a success as far as Susan is concerned. At twenty-two, she looks back with bitterness upon her early life and still cannot bring herself to like the man who tried so hard to buy her affection.

Jane
Along with several brothers and sisters Jane had been brought up in institutions and by foster parents ever since the break-up of her parents' marriage. She in particular had suffered badly at the hands of an unsuitable set of foster parents, and so when her father wrote and said that he was going to remarry and would like all his children to gather round again, she was the one who, at fifteen, decided she would like to go home, the others being happy to stay where they were. She arrived home whereupon Dad said 'Jane, meet Pat; Pat, meet Jane', and that was her sole introduction to the woman who was to try to be her mother. To her horror, Jane soon discovered that she could not communicate with Pat at all, because her step-mother was totally incapable of putting together a few sentences and talking about things. Jane was and still is an extremely friendly and sociable girl. She was simply dying to communicate on a friendly basis, she asked no more of life. A tense situation built up over the next few weeks as Jane became more and more frustrated and in the end she resorted to the violence she had known in her earlier life and stabbed her new mother with a kitchen knife.

Although this is an extreme example it illustrates what can happen when there is no casual meeting and little opportunity of gradually building up a relationship before the introduction of the remarriage concept.

Introducing the Idea of Remarriage
After you and the children have had a chance to get to know one another the time will come to introduce the idea of remarriage to the children. Marriage, parenthood and a new formation of the family unit is a large step forward from mere friendship and needs handling carefully. You will need to choose the right moment and your approach to the problem will vary according to the age-group of the children involved.

I think the first mention of marriage is best made in the absence of the prospective step-parent, in fairness to both parties. The natural parent is the common link between you and the children and it is important for him/her to gauge their response to the news. The children will then get the chance to react spontaneously without feeling inhibited in front of a new parent-figure.

Where there is a good relationship between the natural parent and children, they, the children, should be involved fully in the decision to remarry. By this I do not mean that the parent should ask their children's permission, which would impose further burdens on the children, but should take them into their confidence and explain all the reasons for wanting to remarry. After all, the children are going to be very much involved in this marriage, it is not just a contract between two people, as in the usual case. It is important that the parent should be frank and not 'whitewash' anything. If, for instance, he or she is lonely, why not say so? This is a feeling the children have probably experienced too and can sympathize with. Why not put forward all the reasons why he/she loves this second partner? Let the children be aware of these qualities and love them too. If children are taken into their parent's confidence in this way, I think they are more likely to respond in an adult manner and stand by their parent's choice, even though perhaps not completely sharing the same views.

It is vital too to have ready answers for all the questions a child might ask after hearing such important news. Don't be surprised if the questions are not so momentous as you anticipated. Questions such as 'Will I still be able to keep my tortoise?' or 'Can we still have fish and chips every Friday night?' will come as a welcome relief no doubt, but they will nevertheless indicate to you that your children want their life to remain as normal after the. 'event'. They will want to be reassured on every issue and will be quick to sense any hesitance on the part of their parent, so be prepared!

How not to tell your child about remarriage:

a) Never introduce the idea of marriage without a satisfactory preliminary period of gradual acquaintance, for children as well as adults need time to adjust to a new situation.
b) Never let the children think that because you have chosen another partner, the former parent has to be erased from their

lives. Their feelings on this matter must be respected even if they differ from yours. Make it abundantly clear that the new partner is *your* choice and that although you want very much for the children to love their step-parent, you are not expecting an immediate transfer of filial affection.

c) Beware of giving the impresssion that a 'replacement' is required, such as a spare part for a car. This would be unfair on the second partner and would implant the wrong sort of feelings in the child. Remarks such as: 'We need a mum to clean the house/do the dishes/make the beds' or 'I've got to have a man about the house, to do the repairs and pay all these bills we can't afford' are definitely not on. It is most important for the natural parent to stress that this new partner is loved and wanted as a life-long companion, not just as someone who will temporarily fill a gap in the existing family structure.

Younger children
When the children are too young to understand the 'man to man' approach, the same things must be said, but at their own level. Try to relate to their kind of world, using their kind of words. If you know of a step-family nearby or among family friends, use this as an example. Point out how happy and 'normal' they all are. Say that you would never have known that Mr X is not the children's real daddy, for example. If you have already managed to talk successfully to an older child about the event, perhaps he can explain it to his younger brother or sister better than you can.

Actually, the common opinion among step-parents I have talked to is that the younger the children are, the easier they find it to accept a new parent, so long as they are absolutely assured of their happy little life remaining so. It is up to you therefore to show them lots of love at this time and never to let them think for a moment that they are going to be pushed into the background by the new arrival. Happiness and love are like soft butter, easy to spread, so make sure that both of you share these feelings with the children.

Babies and toddlers
This must be the easiest of age-groups to take on as step-children.

A baby has no preconceived ideas about step-parents, it only perceives warmth and love in general and should soon take to a new parent so long as that love is expressed. Babies and toddlers haven't had years of training and do not need wordy explanations so they can more quickly adapt to a few new ways where necessary.

So far we have discussed getting to know your new family before you actually unite as such. The first step was to meet on a casual basis until you felt you all knew each other well enough to take the second step, that of introducing the idea of a remarriage. This idea will take a while to establish itself in the children's minds and you should try not to rush things at this stage. Remember always that they have not asked to be part of a second marriage, that if under age they have little option but to stay with the parent in whose custody they have been placed, and that they are human beings just as much as you are. So however anxious you both are to embark on your step-marriage, hold back if possible in order to let the third natural stage of getting to know each other take place.

Building on the Foundation
After you have laid the foundations of friendship and trust and have told the children of your intentions, there will follow a period before you marry which can be put to very good use in building up the relationships already begun.

Since your aim is now to unite as a family it is a good idea to 'practise' for the eventuality. In other words, think up, together with your partner, some situations which might help create a 'family' atmosphere but do try not to make them terribly obvious and laboured. For instance, decide upon an activity or outing which would appeal to all of you, such as a trip on a pleasure boat, a mixed activity day at a leisure centre, a visit to the local swimming baths and so on. Then round off the occasion with a meal out at a café. Eating out together will be fun in itself and as joint parents you and your partner will be able to assume very naturally those separate duties which mother and father have on these occasions. Simple things such as pouring out the tea or milk, helping the little one to eat, or booking the table and paying the bill can unite you as a 'family' and give you all some idea of what the 'real thing' will feel like.

You can gradually extend the amount of time you spend as a 'family', the ultimate being a short holiday together, preferably on neutral ground so that everyone feels equally at ease. My own family discovered a lot of things about each other through the medium of a camping holiday. We didn't always like what we discovered, I hasten to add, but it prepared us for the future and though we were aware that there would be certain clashes of character to come, we also knew that there would be lots of fun and good times together.

Do your best to work at the 'family events' before you take the really big step of marriage. You can discuss them afterwards with your partner and find ways of improving on awkward patches encountered. Gradually you will build up your confidence all round until you all feel ready to live under one roof.

The Integration of Two Families

So far we have talked as though all step-families consist of a natural parent with one or more children in their custody plus one other adult who has no children. Of course, this is not always the case. Sometimes two parents unite and each bring children into the household. If you and your partner are in this position, have you thought about things from the children's point of view or are you still boggling at the fact that you are expected to cope with two ill-assorted families? There is so much happening to you at the moment that it is easy to forget that the children have feelings too and are probably also at a very vulnerable age where apparently trivial incidents can be built up into major issues at the drop of a hat. The guidelines previously outlined still apply to what I will call the 'double step-marriage', but of course it is going to be twice as hard to follow them through since both sets of children will have to come to terms with each other as well as with a new parent.

It will not be easy to engineer casual meetings between the two families without some or all of the children realizing that something is afoot, but do give it a try. If there are several children it is a good idea to arrange for one or two at a time to be involved in the outings, varying the combinations according to the type of outing and their particular hobbies or activities. They will compare notes among themselves, you can be sure, and you can gradually build towards getting all of you together when you judge the time to be right. This plan is obviously not foolproof but for those of you who think it is a feasible proposition, I would recommend it. Perhaps the kind of event best suited to mingling everyone together would be a party where you all invite your friends, or go along to a barbecue or disco where the children can remain safely anonymous if they wish. Try to avoid a formal gathering at this introductory stage; it could become quite oppressive.

The children are sure to see through your attempts at casual meetings at a very early stage, so be ready to tell them of your ultimate intentions even if you haven't managed to give them much time together. They would much rather hear the news from you and your partner than be kept guessing. If each parent decides to talk about remarriage to his own children, this must be done simultaneously so that there is no risk of any child springing the news on one of the other children who is still blissfully unaware of the changes afoot. A tactless or cruel remark from a child can do a lot of damage at this stage. The third stage of the plan we talked of earlier can then proceed, that of getting everyone 'family-orientated'.

I am going to select three qualities now from the many which you will gradually be acquiring, whether you are aware of it or not: sympathy, frankness and the ability to communicate. These three all have an important bearing on how you both handle the double step-marriage.

Sympathy

Sympathy involves feeling for someone, sensing their own feelings and acting accordingly so as not to hurt them. It has already been mentioned that the children involved in step-marriages neither ask nor choose to be involved. You two adults have made a choice and are therefore responsible for whoever else you have brought into your remarriage. Try to put yourselves in their positions or, as Diana Davenport in *One Parent Families* says, 'project yourself under [their] skin'. Look at things through their eyes, bearing in mind their limited experience of life, and you will soon gain an extra dimension of understanding.

Let sympathy for the childrens' position in your remarriage be foremost in your mind now as you take the huge step of juggling two families and a new partner. But do not let it develop into over-indulgence or self-sacrifice. I have met one or two step-parents who went absolutely overboard with the sympathy and paid so much attention to the children's feelings that their partners actually began to feel neglected and pushed aside. More of this later . . .

Frankness
By frankness I mean openness and honesty. Each parent knows his own children very well indeed, and can help his partner along the road to understanding them by being absolutely open about all their annoying little tricks, their bad habits, their redeeming points and their behaviour patterns in general.

The trouble with integrating two sets of children is that they will have separate sets of standards which may not necessarily 'gel' together when the family is under one roof. If you, as parents, are already aware of these personal qualities and standards, at least you will be forearmed before the battle.

You will also need to be frank about your own attitudes towards bringing up children, as the following example shows. Peter had four children and Sheila had three, all within the age group of eleven to seventeen. Peter had not spent much time training his children to be responsible young people: he thought they would turn out fine in the end whether he interfered or not. He certainly didn't like the word 'discipline'. Sheila on the other hand had raised her children to be ready to take responsibility, to know the meaning of courtesy and 'give and take'. Once the family united under one roof the children clashed constantly, there were complaints of unfair treatment — 'Why does *he* get away with that and not me?' — and Sheila soon wore herself out running about after the four uncooperative members of the family, in an effort to keep the peace and give the marriage a chance. 'I was nothing more than an unpaid skivvy', she told me, and after two years left her husband along with his four children to 'stew in their own juice' and see how they managed without her for a time. It was a brave decision and Peter gradually confessed his inadequacies as a child-rearer and begged her to return, promising better things.

Sheila confided to me that she had really wanted a year or two in which to get to know the other family and to mix the two together before settling in to marriage but Peter had been bullheaded, she had been weak, and the rest you know. Sheila had no idea about Peter's views regarding the upbringing of children until they became irrevocably apparent and this example highlights the need for frankness in a relationship if it is to work successfully.

Communication

Once the idea of living together as a family has been introduced, you can begin to do some straight talking to those children old enough to understand. Suppose, for instance, that your future step-son cannot abide soppy, sentimental girls and this description fits your daughter exactly? The two are going to be obliged to live under the same roof, eat together every day etc, so it would be much better, instead of adopting a 'hoping for the best' attitude, to have a good talk to all concerned, not necessarily together, and deliver a little lecture about give and take and tolerance. There is no reason why the children's characters should change miraculously overnight to suit other parties so the accent must be on consideration for others, helpfulness, compromise, etc.

In some circumstances it will do no harm for all the children to be gathered solemnly together in the presence of both parents and have the likely difficulties of family unity set before them quite openly. In this way, both 'sets' of children will hear the same words, everyone will know that this pep-talk is not for them alone and they might at best feel a sense of pulling together for the common good. Do stress if you opt for any of these 'pep-talks' that by 'good' you do mean happiness all round, family togetherness and so on, lest they all enter the marriage with a sense of foreboding, thinking they are expected to be perfection itself. Always speak highly of family fun, joint activities etc. when outlining your reasons for give and take, and be ready to answer all their queries; after all these children have a great part to play in this family and their opinions and feelings do matter.

If you can begin your 'double marriage' on such an open basis of frankness and communication all round, it bodes well for the future.

Time to Think

If you have been adapting the above guidelines to your own situation and have been using your preparation time before marriage to incorporate some of the ideas outlined, it would be a good thing now that you are ready to take the more practical steps to sit down quietly and reflect on what you have already achieved.

A point will have been reached at this stage where preliminaries are about to give way to practicalities which must be undertaken on a far more committed level. These practicalities will be discussed in the following chapter but before you go on, ask yourself a few honest questions.

Do you still feel the same way about your future husband or wife after this period of working up towards family unity? Do you still give each other surprises, treats and presents, have silly moments together, enjoy outings together and so on? If the answer (and do be honest!) is no, then it's better to broach the subject bravely with your partner-to-be before it's too late. It is easy to understand how your initial 'wooing' period might have trailed off into mechanical everyday existence and I think most stepparents would readily sympathize with you, having felt something akin to it themselves. That extra dimension to your marriage, the already-present children, can tend to put the damper on your spontaneity with your partner, particulary if this is your own first marriage. You want to feel gay and flippant but feel you must calm down and prepare for heavy responsibilities, both financial and domestic.

The best thing to do is to confide in your partner, who has probably been feeling the same way, and work out what has gone wrong. If it is literally a question of children under your feet, make a determined effort to farm them out now and then so that you can enjoy time alone together. This was another of Peter and Sheila's problems; wherever they went there would be two or three hangers-on and Peter never noticed the effect this was having on Sheila, who began to feel unloved, not 'special' any more.

An important question to ask yourself at this juncture is 'Does my partner want me for myself or to fulfil a function within his/her family?' Make sure you give yourself an honest answer to this vital question and if you are uncertain give the whole thing lots more time.

Are you perfectly sure, conversely, of your own motives for marrying into a family? If you have a kind, sympathetic, impulsive nature, it could possibly lead you into the role of hero or heroine gallantly going to the rescue of the poor struggling single parent with the adorable children. You may feel wonderfully fulfilled at the time but what about later when you realize there is no real lasting love between the two of you?

You might, on the other hand, feel sure that what you are about to do is right, but be unsure whether you are fitted for it. For instance, I had great difficulty envisaging myself being cosy and motherly, tending the sick, feeding the hungry, doing four lots of filthy washing, putting zips in jeans, etc. yet somehow knew in my bones that I was doing the right thing. If this sounds familiar, perhaps a course of marriage guidance counselling would benefit either or both of you. The counsellors have a wealth of knowledge and experience at their fingertips and can help you through the next stage of your planning. They are trained advisers who won't guarantee to solve all your problems by waving a magic wand, but they will get you talking, they will help you clear your mind of unnecessary clutter (referred to, by a counsellor friend of mine, as the 'luggage' you take with you into a second marriage). You will also discover after talking to them that you are only one of thousands in a similar situation who all come with the same doubts and questions. Don't think, therefore, that you have to be in a desperate plight before you talk to them; they will find it much easier to advise at this stage and you might find you are able to jettison some of that luggage and feel much lighter for it!

Case Histories

Standards

'There were lots of immediate changes, stricter rules'. Tim was used to a liberal upbringing and when his step-mother came on the scene he could not easily accept the different standards she set. She liked a fixed meal-time and would set the table nicely and expect a family gathering. He was used to rummaging in the kitchen at any hour of the day or lounging in front of the television with a hamburger.

June saw her half of the family (four children) as 'coming over worse' with respect to behaviour. Her step-brother and sister, she said, were too well brought up: 'there is still a barrier, we are not on the same wavelength. Caroline and James had such different backgrounds. James was just too polite for my liking, leaping to open doors ahead of me etc. It was all too much, he was just too good. I got cross and tried talking but it was no good; I kept him at arm's length and treated him with disdain.'

Preparation

Dave's father, a widower, took each of his five children aside and explained to them that he was getting on (60) and didn't want to be a burden to his children; he had met a lady who wanted to care for a family and would make life much easier for himself and the children.

'He asked us all if we agreed to the idea of his remarriage, then deliberately left the situation as it was for six months in order to give us time to reconsider. We all approved.'

Tim, now nineteen, is bitter about the way in which his father broached the idea of remarriage: 'It was slily announced; second-hand information. I think it was a very bad thing to do. I could have been kept informed of the build-up to the split and that Dad had a girlfriend. I could have coped with it. I felt I was not considered enough. I found a step-mother in my home on my return from boarding school. The regulations for access were set up *before* I got home. My father's motives behind his building up for me an idyllic picture of a new life with a nice stepmother were OK but it was all too soon, he didn't let things settle, very bad timing'.

'It was really a fait accompli, it didn't matter what the children thought about the remarrriage. They could have been more open about things, given more warning about events. I know I could have handled the situation, young though I was.'

Tom got to know his stepfather first as a friend of the family. 'I think things might have been better if I had got to know him as a future father-figure instead. Maybe I could have started off on the right footing then'.

'I think Dad assembled the three of us to tell us about the change in custody and remarriage. Then there was a period of living as a family under one roof at my future grandparents, including a holiday together, so this provided a way of getting used to our future step-mother and an idea of what family life would eventually be like'.

'I remember a few outings to the zoo, all of us, and to budgie and guinea-pig shows.' These were subjects which interested the whole family, including the future step-father.

Many children reported that their new parent figures had moved in

PLANNING: PRELIMINARIES

whilst they were at boarding school or that their own parent had moved into another home.

'I was very angry when father wrote to tell me that a step-mother would move in when the house had been redecorated. "I'm not having anyone coming into *my* house" was what I thought.'

'I was moved out of my home in my absence. I wasn't involved in it. Our house was completely emptied. Everything was moved to the other home. I felt very disturbed; you really haven't got your own ground to stand on any more, you're in someone else's domain.'

'We didn't get to know straightaway about Dad's remarriage. I thought it was wrong to hear it after everyone else.'

'I was told of the marriage plan in a very matter of fact way: "Joan and I have decided to get married". I think you should break the child in gently before discussing the possibility of marriage. In my case, two meetings were not enough, even though one of them was a fortnight's holiday.'

2.

PLANNING: PRACTICALITIES

You have now reached the stage in your preparations where decisions have to be taken on a much more committed level; the preliminaries give way to practicalities. You have hopefully sorted out your ideas about upbringing, family life, and so on, and have done your best to help all the children involved in your remarriage to a good understanding of the situation.

With this part of your planning safely behind you, you can now look ahead with confidence to a new way of living and get to grips with a few further questions which must be dealt with before your marriage. Some of them will appear to be major issues, some might not affect you at all, so as with the previous chapter they will be discussed in no particular order of importance and you will be able to select and discuss those which apply to your own situation.

A Fresh Start
Should you move away from your present area when you marry or not? Will you be harming the children's education by uprooting them? Can you stand losing good friends and neighbours at a time when you feel you need them most? Will the grandparents be able to accept the move? How can you be sure what the future holds for you in a new home in a new district? These and a host of other questions begin to buzz around your head when this subject arises — I know from experience! Panic can set in unless you get together with your partner and draw up a list of pros

and cons to be talked over methodically and quietly. I am going to put forward my own list to help get you going, and from my points you will be able to move naturally on to your own particular reasons for or against a move.

Pros:
1. *Interference*
You have the task ahead of you of building up a warm family unit out of unrelated people. You will all live very closely together under the same roof from the moment you marry your partner and will be expected by the public at large to behave like a normal family. You don't yet know for sure how the children are going to react to you both in this situation and will need time and space to concentrate on your efforts. The presence of 'ex-parents', grandparents, aunts or uncles, etc. on your doorstep is not going to help the situation for, however kindly meant, interference will occur and you have enough to do coping with your new position without having to handle relatives too.

They remember the 'old ways' of the previous parent and you as new parent and partner will naturally have 'new ways' of your own. These new ways have to be carefully and sensitively introduced to avoid unnecessary conflict. Just imagine having to pacify your relatives at the same time as juggling your new, more personal relationships — clashes are inevitable, and I think that a certain distance between the old family and the new can be a good thing. It has been thought by many to actually help towards improving relationships all round.

2. *'I'm going to tell my Dad!'*
Children are quick to make comparisons when they feel that things have changed for the worse. It is all too easy to run down the road to their 'real Dad' and pour out their sob story, embellishing it here and there with a touch of melodrama. 'Real Dad' will not be quite certain how much of this saga to believe and will also find it very difficult to send the child right back with a sharp reminder that they are to do as their new parent says in the home. Liz, one of the many step-children I have chatted to, told me how she was forever comparing her new father with her 'real Dad', often to his face, and running off to her natural father, who lived nearby, as soon as things didn't go her way. Thus the

new parent was up against the odds and the old was placed in an awkward position; a common problem which a change of address can often solve with minimum aggravation on all sides.

3. Reminders of the past

You are trying to build up a future together but with so many reminders of the past around you if you stay in the same house or district, is this going to be possible? If you simply move into your partner's home where he or she has lived perhaps for years with the person you are 'replacing' as it were, is this going to help you start a new life together? Will you feel like a guest or employee rather than master or mistress in your own home? How will you feel, as a new wife, surrounded by furnishings, bedding, tea-cups, etc. all chosen by another woman? What about the new husband who cannot help but notice all the evidence of male handiwork around the house, a legacy of his wife's past he would prefer to forget. A home which is new to both of you would solve these irritations.

4. A change of air

A change of environment is like a holiday, it refreshes you, recharges your batteries and makes you see life with fresh eyes. You can more easily forget the unpleasant things which have been happening to you and actually *feel* that you have made a fresh start in life. Also, imagine for a moment that after much self-questioning you have decided that you ought to change your ways in some respects; perhaps you feel you have been too proud in the past, or too lenient. It is very difficult, as we all know, to alter overnight and present a new 'you' to your friends and relatives. You might be laughed at, stared at, your pride might be hurt and all your good intentions will fly out of the window as you see that it will never work because people won't give you a chance. If this sounds familiar, a move away could solve the problem wonderfully, for no one will know the 'old you' when you settle in a new neighbourhood. Only your partner will know and he or she can only be full of appreciation for the efforts you are making. Think about it — a clean slate is much easier to achieve when you don't feel self-conscious under the scrutiny of acquaintances and relatives.

Cons:

1. *Financial security*

You may be financially secure in your present position. If you move, what are the chances of finding a new job, a suitable home near suitable schools and finding the funds for it all? This is an important question, particularly in these days of rising costs, difficulties with housing transactions, and unemployment. Since you are already taking a step in the dark with your new family commitments dare you also run the risk of a similar step regarding these other factors? Our own family was fortunate enough to move to a tied cottage which went with a perfect job, but how many others can count on such luck?

2. *Schooling*

Schooling is the next question to consider. What are the age groups of your children and how are they likely to be affected by a change of school? A child, particularly after any upset such as a divorce or a bereavement, needs security, a regular dependable pattern of life, the assurance that certain things will always remain the same. Ask your children's headmaster or class teachers what their opinions are and without alarming your offspring, try to test out their reactions to the possibility. We feel that our two eldest at fourteen and fifteen suffered initially from the uprooting but that the youngest, aged ten, took no harm at all.

3. *Adaptability*

How adaptable is your new family? How much do roots and friendships and all things dear and familiar mean to you? Are you prepared to give them up and take a chance on starting again from scratch? True friends will always remain so despite distance, and fast motorways can soon shorten a journey back to visit all your old haunts, but if you are really daunted at the prospect of leaving your home background, it is no use trying to be brave and to fool yourself into thinking you can cope; it will only lead to further heartache and stress.

4. *A question of guilt*

Guilt is a complex subject on which I am not qualified to expound.

However, the word 'step-parent' still has attached to it the stigma of guilt, even in this so-called enlightened age. People like to assume there must be a guilty party involved, or a shadowy past lurking somewhere behind a step-marriage. The reasons for this are not in question here, but the effect can be to make you *feel* guilty when there is no need. The fact that a step-family has moved house might be viewed by those left behind as an admission of guilt, a fleeing from the murky past. Are you prepared to have this accusation levelled at you? You might also encounter similar suspicions when you arrive in your new area so it's worth a thought before you make your decision. Personally, I'm in favour of the old saying: 'sticks and stones may break my bones but words can never hurt me', but it doesn't do for all of us.

The decision concerning a fresh start is a big one, there is no doubt about it. What I would advise you to do is read through the above points bearing in mind your own circumstances, weigh up your own extra pros and cons, and having reached a decision, work out how to prepare your children for it. Make sure that they don't get what I shall call the 'package deal treatment'. They must never be allowed to feel that their feelings have not been considered, that they are dragged along as part and parcel of whatever you choose to do. They will mostly be concerned about close friends and relatives being left behind if your decision is to move away, and will be bothered about all manner of strange (to you) little worries such as whether there will be any fishing near the new abode, or whether there will be a roller skating rink. These things are very important to the children even if they do look trivial compared with your worries so you must have answers at the ready and plenty of reassurance to hand.

Summing up the question of a fresh start, I would say that the general concensus of opinion is that a completely new start in a different home, if not a new area, is the best thing, thus ensuring that no one of you feels disadvantaged from the very beginning. If financial difficulties will not permit a change of home, then at least make provision for the new residents to make their own impression on the place and show understanding of their desire to remove all evidence of the past. This problem is discussed in more depth on page 72, as it is one area which appears to cause much suffering, particularly among step-mothers.

Access

This is the subject which appears to attract the most attention publicly. How often do we read headlines in the newspapers about 'tugs of love', and 'snatchings' of offspring outside the school gates? The press love it and the public gobble it up eagerly, sympathizing readily with the pathetic figure knocking on the door, bag of sweets in one pocket, new dolly in the other, coming to claim his poor little girl for the miserable few hours which have been granted him legally. Resentful mother is pictured opening the door a crack and pushing out the child with a 'don't be late back' remark and a slam in father's face. These things can and do happen and in the following chapters advice and help will be offered, but here we are talking about planning and preparing, so let's think about ways in which you can maybe obviate some of the problems before they can occur.

If there has been no divorce in your case, or if the 'ex-parent' does not show interest in visiting or keeping in touch, you can count yourself lucky, but in the vast majority of step-families these days there is a question of access to contend with. Peter Rowlands' book *Saturday Parent* is excellent on this subject and I would recommend everyone to read it and, if possible, keep a copy at hand for future reference. I cannot deal with the question as fully as he does but we can at least set down some guidelines for discussion.

Whom is 'access' meant to benefit?

Basically it is designed to help the non-custodial parent and the child living within the step-family to keep a relationship which they have been judged a right to have. That it doesn't always work out as simply as this will be discussed in Chapter 5. On this reasoning, therefore, the custodial parent and step-parent should keep in the background and allow the meetings to take place in as pleasant and easy an atmosphere as possible. If the non-custodial parent has been granted a certain pattern of access legally, you would do well to accept this fact and make the very best of it. It will help to look at it from the standpoint of all others involved and you will soon realize that they too are not totally happy about the situation — the child feels torn between his two parents and the visitor feels embarrassed and awkward.

Continuity and security

If the child or children in a step-family-to-be are already used to a regular pattern of visiting and/or outings with their other natural parent do plan to keep to this pattern where possible when you join with your new partner. There is enough going on at this moment to disturb the children without further upheaval. As Ruth Inglis says in her book *Must Divorce Hurt the Children?* 'keep the child's world as intact as possible'. Regular visits will perhaps not do a great deal for you, but they let the child know that life is still going on as usual.

Plan ahead

If it is possible in your case it will greatly help at this stage to discuss with the non-custodial parent just what form his/her access can best take. This way you can try to ensure the maximum benefit and the minimum hurt, for there is no denying that there is going to be a mixture of both with so many factors to be taken into consideration.

Even if you appear to be 'getting away with it' (for example, if you are moving right away and have not heard from the non-custodial parent recently) prepare yourselves for the possibility that he/she might have a change of mind and press for access, or your children might conceivably decide they miss their natural parent sorely and need to see them. Work out a good plan together; you will feel happier about the situation if you have faced up to it and are in control.

Remember finally that as the years go by, situations change, children alter, parents remarry, begin new lives and so on, and your present difficulties could easily be dissolved in the near future.

Finances

Although money is by no means as important as love in your marriage, it is a sensible person who sits down and takes stock with his or her partner before leaping blindly into the delights of second marriage.

Maintenance payments

These spring to mind readily as soon as divorce proceedings are concluded. It is worth checking with your solicitor on this subject, making sure that you understand any commitments that have been undertaken. Since the laws concerning maintenance are constantly subject to change I do not propose to go into details here, but you can easily drop in on your local Citizens' Advice Bureau who will be able to give you information or refer you to a specialist. Maintenance payments are another bone of contention which frequently cause trouble for step-families. If you have obligations which are beyond your means now, the State can intervene at your request and, after reviewing your finances, can give welfare support, so do not worry unduly on this score.

If, however, you find you must continue to make maintenance payments, are you going to be able to live with your new family unit on the level you would like? Will you resent this flow of money from your household towards someone you would perhaps rather forget? It is perfectly natural to answer yes and at this stage of your planning you ought to consider your reaction and prepare yourself for it.

To work or not to work?
If you are to be a step-mother as opposed to a step-father, it may be financially necessary to consider whether you will have to work once you are married. You are taking on a great deal, becoming mother to someone else's children at the same time as learning to live with your new husband. It might be a good idea to give up work for a year or so until you have mastered your new role in life but if you have no choice in the matter now is the time to work out how you can best organize things so that you can cope without either wearing yourself down or seeing your family suffer. Look into ways of obtaining work at home or working the hours best suited to the ages of the children. A useful book to read on this point is *How to Survive as a Working Mother* by Lesley Garner. It gives many practical suggestions and is full of handy names and addresses as well as information on tax benefits and so on. Well worth a read!

Remember, as already mentioned, that circumstances will alter, ex-spouses will remarry or drift away and you will not be burdened forevermore with the financial load you might now see looming before you. One other point to remember — your husband will not be exactly happy at having to share out his income between two households so bear this in mind when you talk it over and be sympathetic, it will help enormously!

Starting a New Family

Before getting married most couples ask themselves what size of family they would like to have, how long they will wait before they start it, etc. and naturally enough these will be questions that also apply to you and your partner. Just because there is a ready-made family it doesn't mean you can't add to it!

Time and again I am asked 'Didn't you have any of your own?' to which I patiently reply that as far as I am concerned, our three *are* my own — I was given them by my husband as a wedding present! However, I know that I am in the minority when it comes to this question. Most step-mums who are young enough want to have at least one child 'of their own'. I think this is partly to make them feel 'normal' and partly to weld the two sides of the family together, particularly where there are already children from both. I remember one particular mum who told me they had held a family pow-wow, the children on both sides being old enough to be involved, and had voted unanimously for a new baby. The little boy holding her hand as she spoke was the result of that decision, and had indeed brought the family to closer unity.

The only drawbacks in starting a new family are that jealousies might arise if there is any favouritism, which you must be on the lookout for in advance, and that an extra mouth to feed means less money to share around.

The 'Step' Syndrome — Choosing a Name

Recently an acquaintance of mine rang me up and one of my boys answered the phone in my absence. When I saw her next she asked, 'Did you get my message, one of your step-sons answered the phone?' The use of the prefix 'step' somehow grated on me, it sounded like someone I didn't have any connection with, not Michael, our youngest. Of course, she was probably being cautious, not knowing me very well, yet aware that I was a step-mum and hoping she was using the correct term. I didn't mind but it gave me food for thought. A difference was implied, wasn't it? Things were not quite normal in our family apparently. I had never called our boys 'step-sons' when speaking of them to her but she had evidently set me aside as someone a bit different from the average mother. I was quite taken aback as I hadn't seen myself in that light before.

Similarly, I was telling a friend that I was doing some research on step-parents and after quite some time he happened to mention that he himself had an adopted son and was having one or two problems with him in adolescence. He then let slip that actually it was his wife's child and he had married her when the baby was very tiny. Surprised, I blurted out 'Then you are a step-parent too, aren't you?' and watched it dawn on him that yes, how silly of him, that was right. He simply hadn't thought of himself under such a title, he had just assumed the role of father and had got on with the job. So you see, step-parents don't always think of themselves as a class apart from normal parents and I would imagine that in some cases, the constant reference to oneself as *step*-parent could be quite hurtful.

What about the children? Will they mind being introduced as someone's step-sons or step-daughters? I would say that in a large percentage of cases, yes, they are very sensitive on this subject. Children do not like to look or feel any different from their peers. They like the safe anonymity of conforming to whatever style of hair or dress is in fashion, and they copy the current slang and catch-phrases. You just try and send your daughter to school in flat shoes when all her friends are wearing small heels and you will know what I mean, even if you cannot remember your own childhood pains.

Introductions and references are likely to cause you possible embarrassment if you are at all sensitive to the use of the word 'step', so be prepared to hear your official title given to you now and then. It may occur when you are filling in forms, or visiting the doctor with your child for instance, or when you happen to be far too young to be natural mum to the gangling youth at your side. You will find yourself having to explain when eyebrows shoot up in surprise, which can be a chore at times but most people react swiftly with a very pleasant rewarding remark on the child's behaviour etc. so don't worry about this aspect at all.

I would recommend consulting your step-children-to-be on the subject of names if they are old enough. If they have a preference why not respect it? It is best sorted out now to save possible embarrassment to either party later, particularly in the case of the children. Mine introduce me as 'their mother' but never use that term when talking to me in general so you might find that you will get a mixture of titles too.

What will they call me?

I have talked to many step-parents about this and they have come up with an amazing variety of answers when asked what their step-children call them. It's a good thing to find out what they would feel most comfortable with — as a mature adult you can adapt to a name you are not particularly keen on rather than force a child to call you a certain name when it doesn't come naturally to him. It will help the child's relationship with you if he feels at home with the word he chooses.

The choice of name seems to lie between some form of mother, mum, mummy, etc. (likewise, of course, with father); your actual Christian name, or a pet name used with affection. Please don't think that if the children don't want to call you mother or father that your prospects as successful step-parent are doomed — this is a common misconception. I have never been given that name myself yet I know that I am treated as an ordinary parent and that is all that really matters. Why should they be forced or even expected to use a term for you which they have been accustomed to using for someone else?

One step-mother I chatted to told me of the day her step-daughter first called her 'Mummy', after months of avoiding calling her anything. She had wept with joy as she wrote the fact in her diary, viewing it as a real breakthrough in their relationship. One divorcee I spoke to told me that after her husband left home her seven-year-old daughter said 'I haven't got a Daddy now, have I?' She let this ride for a while then after hearing it once too often replied 'Yes of course you have, it's just that he doesn't live here any more'. The child agreed that yes, she had a father but not a *Daddy* which was quite a penetrating comment for a seven-year-old. When the mother remarried it was with fear and trepidation that she waited to hear what formula would be given to the step-father. It was with great relief that she heard the term Daddy used with no prompting whatsoever.

Teenage children might plump for your full Christian name, feeling that this is grown up and suitable. If it goes against the grain with you, you can mention the fact, but do not try to make them change if they really feel comfortable with the usage. It doesn't have to imply familiarity, distance or contempt or whatever else you imagine; try to tolerate whatever you are given and remember that it could change as the months tick by and they become more used to family life with you.

The children may prefer to use an affectionate name and in this category I find myself. I don't propose to set down all the ones I have been blessed with in the past, you might only laugh, but now after thirteen years it has simply settled down to a shortened version of my Christian name — Chrissie I am and always will be, and I don't mind in the least.

So be prepared to accept any of these three types of name given you and remember to take notice of your children's behaviour towards you rather than the words they use to address you. After all, it is feelings which count most. Remember too that as youngsters grow up, so attitudes and ideas change, and you might even receive the variety of names I have enjoyed over the years.

Surnames

When Mum remarries and takes her children with her, are they to keep the name they were born with or change it to their new father's name, as she will? I don't see any particular merit in either choice — again it will be a matter to discuss before you marry. If the family is old enough, put it to them and see how they feel.

Two factors spring to mind which influence the decision. First, the children might feel 'different' if they have a different name from their parents and we have already talked about children's feelings on this subject. Secondly, their natural father might have objections to a change of surname and in this case you would have to seek professional advice. I know of one case where the natural father objected to the adoption of his son by the step-father, but the boy simply assumed the new name in any case so they reached a kind of compromise.

The Wedding

All this talk of names brings us nicely now to the event you have been building up towards during your planning and 'practising' time — your wedding and immediate unity as a family. I do hope that you feel by now that it has been worth while delaying the event until you have given yourselves and your children time to get accustomed to the idea. I have met so many step-parents in distress who really regretted rushing into the event before they and their family-to-be were quite prepared for it. Much bitterness can be avoided and a great deal of heartache saved by holding back until you feel you are completely ready and raring to go!

Please do not fall into the trap set for you by general public opinion (that anonymous but powerful influence) that your or your partner's second marriage is somehow second rate and should be undertaken quietly and furtively with minimum public attention. This cannot possibly help towards the good start which your marriage deserves after all the effort you have put into the preliminaries. I can only beg you to be bold and have the type of wedding you really want, with your friends, relatives *and* your new young family present. If you want a white wedding and the church find they cannot accommodate you because of a divorce in the background, you may have to accept the option of a registry office wedding, but don't forget you can still have all the other unforgettable regalia connected with traditional weddings if you wish. Church policy on this subject is in a state of flux so don't simply write off the idea of a 'normal' wedding. It will help enormously to show that you intend to be an ordinary couple with a normal family and don't give two hoots for public opinion. Get in touch with your local church if you are not already a practising member and find out what their policy is.

At this point I cannot help but remember our own wedding thirteen years ago in our local church. The minister, an elderly man whose simple comment about divorce had been 'Who are we to judge', had prepared a special service which allowed for the fact that our three boys were present (sitting safely out of mischief, trapped firmly between two grandparents). He did not miss out any of the usual parts of the wedding service but cleverly adapted his words to include the new family aspect. This marriage was not a thing to hide, it was something to give thanks for and deserved a special blessing. Everybody, including those relatives who had expressed doubt about the boys' presence, said how wonderful the service had been. The boys themselves admitted later to having been somewhat bemused but had not objected at all to sitting in a 'pew of honour' — in fact one of them was all but bursting with laughter at the sight of his Chrissie in flowing white instead of the usual jeans and shirt!

But enough of reminiscing. I mention my own case only to prove to you that a second wedding has every right to be celebrated in the same way as the first and an extra blessing does not go amiss either for such an important undertaking as a step-marriage. A young woman I spoke to remembers being deeply and lastingly hurt by the fact that her father and step-mother did not ask her to their wedding though she was fifteen and would have loved to have been a bridesmaid. She has still never really forgiven them for this act of rejection, even though they all get along together well now after a stormy and traumatic start to family life.

So here is food for thought on the subject of your wedding. Discuss it together and make it the wedding of the year! Don't deny yourselves a honeymoon either unless financial or other circumstances prevent it; grandparents are pretty good at looking after children for a week, as we found out! Self-sacrifice is all well and good up to a point but you could regret missing this one important week of marital bliss for two when you are both immersed in the pains and pleasures of family life.

Case Histories

A fresh start
'The worst violation was being moved out of our house.'

June found she was too far away from her mother at crisis times. 'When it came to the personal problems of growing up I dealt with them alone, apart from crying on the phone to Mum from school. I couldn't take these problems to my step-mother and Mum was too far away always.'

Two brothers, Martin and Mike, both missed their friends initially after the move from their home area and the nice old familiar family home which held 'happy childhood memories'. They both felt they had suffered a little from changing schools at the ages of thirteen and fifteen, particularly Mike who thought he was 'just starting to improve at last' before the move.

Tim chose to live with his mother in her house after his parents' marriage broke up and his father remarried. 'But I missed the childhood home, there were always lots of interesting things to do there. I felt I had made a sacrifice by moving to Mother's. Now that my original home has changed so much under my stepmother's influence, I don't look on it so fondly, however.'

'When we moved house I didn't miss my friends as much as my brother did, I make friends easily. The change of school was quite a shock.'

He changed from a tiny village school to a large comprehensive.

Names

'I avoided giving my step-mother any name at first, then eventually managed the short name everyone used for her.' When phoning home Tim feels awkward and finds it difficult to say 'Is Dad there?' when other family members answer. Instead, he says 'Is Mr Dickenson there?' When speaking to his step-brother he finds it difficult too, having to say things like 'Have you seen *my* Dad?' or 'Where's *your* mother?'

John has to be careful in his choice of words for addressing his step-mother. He calls her Mum to her face but refers to her as Mother in her absence. Apparently she has asked to be called Mum and becomes angry and upset when he makes a slip.

Mike remembers his father asking him to call his new wife Mum, 'but I couldn't and wouldn't'. She then said it didn't matter and the shortened first name was quickly put into use and has remained.

At the age of three, Brian gained a step-father who was introduced by his Christian name and insisted on its use. Brian understood later in life that the man felt inferior to the wartime hero who was his father and did not want the comparison.

'I couldn't call her anything at all, even now.'

Alan has two step-fathers. 'I called my first step-father Dad because I was very young, then changed it to his Christian name later on when things cooled.' He uses the shortened Christian name for his current step-father and the surname he was born with for all official purposes, but finds it no problem, having an easy-going nature.

Surname problems arrived for Chris at school where she had to keep explaining her situation to youngsters and even teachers. 'I needed two consent forms at a time, one for each set of parents. Sometimes, too, my friends can't find me in the telephone book because the phone is in my step-father's name of course, and I use my father's surname.'

'Dad wanted our names to be changed when I was nine' (the children had assumed their stepfather's name and lived with him very happily). 'I was mad and took it out on other people. It's a bit complicated at school with forms, etc. but I don't mind particularly'. Stuart's father obtained a court order to say that they must use their natural surname.

'We asked them [Mum and new husband] what we should call them and they said "What do you want to call us?" We settled for Mum and Philip for them and Dad and Jean for Dad and his new wife. Then there was a discussion before our little sister was born to decide what name she would learn to say to her father. Daddy was decided for her, but now she occasionally slips in Philip as well.'

The wedding

Martin reminisced about being present at his father's wedding with some amusement. He and his two brothers (aged ten to fifteen) were all giggling whilst other relatives were traditionally crying.

'Watching a parent getting married was rather amusing,' he says, but was pleased to see Dad happy again. He remembers the reception 'stuffing all that wedding cake', his new grandad's funny speech and his new uncle's car with lots of gadgets attached.

Caroline's father remarried before her mother did. 'None of us were invited to the wedding. I was angry, though I wouldn't have gone anyway.'

Susan, at about sixteen, was a witness at her father's wedding and spoke of it proudly, pleased to have been involved and considered in this adult way, even though she was not too keen on the idea of his remarriage.

'I was furious at not even being asked whether I should like to attend the wedding — it was assumed I would not'. Paula was fourteen. 'I think parents should at least discuss whether or not the child should attend the wedding; I still feel resentful about that today!' She is now forty.

3.

THE INTERIM PERIOD

The interim period refers to the time which elapses between the death of the natural parent or the divorce or separation, and the moment that you 'inherit' the children as step-parent. What has happened to the children during this period can, I believe, have a very strong bearing on how they react when brought together as a step-family. Make it your business to be aware of who looked after them, what kind of an upbringing they were given, what kind of a routine they were used to. Having a knowledge of their background can help you a great deal when it comes to clashes of personality and behaviour problems during your 'takeover' period.

Sometimes it happens that during the interim period the children live with one distraught parent who has little time to give to them whilst coping with personal problems. They may run wild, taking advantage of the lack of discipline, and losing a lot of the good habits which they have previously learnt. It is hard for a step-parent to take over after a period such as this and though there are no easy answers it is a definite help if you understand *why* the children are difficult to handle now that they are back into a family routine once more. You can take this into consideration when deciding your own policy.

Often the children live with an aunt and uncle or gran and grandad and are spoilt or babied, again making it very difficult for you to bring them back to everyday normal family life. A friend of mine always complains that after a week's holiday at his grandparent's home, her step-son gives her 'absolute hell' on his return because he has got used to being treated as a spoilt little boy and finds he can't take the discipline and stricter life that Lucy believes in. Imagine what she would have to cope with if he had just spent a year with his grandparent, never mind one week!

If the said relatives have enjoyed filling this gap in continuity and rather resent your arrival on the scene, you will meet up with further problems which will demand the utmost tact, since these people have, undeniably, played an important part in the children's upbringing. Make it your business to thank them for all their efforts and perhaps consult them occasionally when sorting out problems, to make them feel important still.

I know of one case where the children, two little girls, lived with their grandmother for many years from the ages of one and three, being virtually brought up by her, and by the time a new mother arrived on the scene, this old lady had indoctrinated them into thinking that their natural mother was a very wicked person who had beaten them, abandoned them and goodness knows what else. One day the girls were confronted by a strange woman at the school gates who announced that she was their own mother and they were terrified, having no personal recollection to go by and only a terrible picture painted by their grandma, which they believed. They fled home to their step-mother, and she had a very difficult time trying to smooth over such a complicated situation. Fortunately, she was well aware of the interim period they had experienced and she succeeded in handling things.

Sometimes it can happen that the one-parent unit manages very well and finds it hard to readjust to yet another way of family life. Doreen, a woman now in her sixties, looks back to the days when she and her elder sister were looking after Dad, after Mother had died. Her sister, at eighteen, was very efficient at coping and everything was going well until there arrived one day out of the blue a very bossy character who announced she was going to be the new mother in the family. She took over swiftly and capably without a thought for the elder sister. This girl was suddenly made redundant, every care and duty was taken from her, and her whole way of life was shattered overnight. The girls' father was to blame, of course, for not gradually introducing his new partner to the children, but the step-mother herself could have made things so much more bearable if she had only realized how well this little trio had been managing before her arrival. A better approach would have been to allow the daughter to continue with various tasks, maybe to consult her about things occasionally, or simply to congratulate her on how well she had managed during the interim period. A 'woman to woman' talk with her step-daughter about their new roles would have been better than simply snatching the reins out of Sheila's hands and overturning the well-run household in one fell swoop.

Children need continuity in their lives and without it they can stray away from their usual course leaving the new parent to tie up the loose ends on 'takeover'. Your first job then, after making yourself familiar with the background of this intervening period, is to provide security by establishing a pattern of family living to which the children can easily adapt. Wean them gently but firmly off their wayward ways using tact and diplomacy, especially if relatives have been looking after them. Above all, give them time to adjust. Remember that their first pattern of life has been disrupted: they have had to adapt to one-parent life, and now you have come along with the best of intentions, expecting them to adapt yet again to your pattern of life. It is a great deal to expect from a child and you must wait patiently for the effects of these disruptions to wear off before you see evidence of your own impact on the family.

Loss and Grief

All step-families are born of loss, a fact which we step-parents would do well to bear in mind. When one parent has died, the individuals left must come to terms with their grief and learn to live without them. The same happens after a divorce; the partner and his or her children have to get used to the absence of the one who has left. Even if a husband and wife realize they would be better off apart, this does not necessarily mean that they do not suffer the pain of loss in certain respects, for they will almost certainly regret the loss of their 'good' times together. The family 'as it used to be' will also be mourned when it is broken by death or divorce.

As a new step-parent, you too will suffer a loss when you give up your freedom to take up your new position, particularly if you have not been married before. Suddenly you are expected to change from an independent, single person to a married person with very particular parental duties, often involving many extra difficulties from the very beginning. Naturally, you might feel resentment, even though you chose of your own free will to marry. The other type of loss you will experience is that of the twosome stage which most couples enjoy during the first year or so of marriage. Most step-parents, particularly those for whom this is the first marriage, feel a deep resentment about this, especially during the difficult times encountered. This subject has already been touched on elsewhere but must be borne in mind during this section too.

Loss and grief takes time to come to terms with, hence the need to be extra-sensitive and sympathetic when setting about the job of 'replacing' a lost partner and parent.

Death

When a partner and parent has died it is obvious that they can no longer physically interfere with your efforts to unite the family. Yet in other ways they can be ever-present because the bereaved family is free to idealize or sanctify the dead person until you feel that you simply cannot hope to compete with this figure of perfection. A thoughtless husband can so easily say something like 'Joan didn't make the children eat cereals', or 'Joan made marvellous chocolate cakes', little realizing how much these remarks can cut to the quick when his second wife is making every effort to bring up the children as she sees fit. The children will display resentment quite naturally as soon as you try to make them do things they don't want to — how easy for them and how understandable to say 'Our Mum would never have made us do that'. Their natural mother is not there to refute it and you are put in a very awkward position indeed.

The only way of coping with this behaviour and swallowing the seemingly endless comments is to prepare yourself for them by understanding in the first place *why* they exist. Eventually you may have to be frank and tell the family that you have heard enough now about those chocolate cakes etc. but, meanwhile, try to be extra-sensitive to the situation for it should gradually improve as time goes by.

Divorce

It is perhaps easier to cope with reminders of the natural parent when a divorce has taken place because you know that there was little love left between the adults, hence the need for separation. This in itself is a comfort, you feel in a stronger position with regard to your partner, but it is still tempting to discredit the natural parent in the eyes of the children when they show resentment and make comparisons. You must not give in to this very natural temptation, for the children did not cause the separation and their love for their natural parent must be allowed to remain intact. Let them discover for themselves any defects in his or her character, but never point them out, even in self-defence. Much is demanded of you during your first year or two of step-family life whilst the children are going through the feelings of anger, sadness, jealousy, etc. which all stem from their initial loss of a parent. Sometimes you will feel you need to be a saint yourself to cope, but if you constantly bear in mind how the children must have felt initially when they lost a parent and an old way of family life, it will help you to realize that they still have a few open wounds which you can help close with loving tolerance and patience.

The advice given in this chapter may seem repetitive but I do think that the previously unmarried step-parent has a great deal to learn with regard to the pain involved in a broken marriage. The sorrow following death can be felt by all, or at least imagined if not experienced, but anyone who has not been through the experience of a marital break-up and divorce cannot fully grasp the sensation of loss. Only through talking to others, for instance, and reading round the subject have I come to realize why so much complicated behaviour seems to follow a divorce. Talk to other people yourself, there are plenty of ordinary men and women among your acquaintances who will not mind opening up on the subject if your interest is genuine. You can even join a local step-parent group where you will find others willing to share experiences and learn how to cope with problems by understanding what has caused them in the first place.

Case Histories

The interim period

June's step-mother was very good to her new family and found a need to buy them new clothes upon 'takeover'. This was not viewed as bribery, says June, she knew her step-mother was too intelligent for that. 'We were scruffy little beggars and needed taking in hand after running a bit wild, all away at school with no firm parental control.' June didn't know how to handle this generosity and knew that her step-mother thought the family ungrateful but says they were not used to it, as they had managed on very little during the interim period.

Martin and Mike look back on the first part of their interim period as their 'riches to rags' time, having moved from a comfortable happy home to not such a nice home without a father in it. Martin in particular was given a rough time by his mother and has 'unhappy memories' of that period. He began to behave badly at school and thinks the absence of their father did not help at this stage. The boys were left alone all night occasionally and twelve years later, still tell the tale of the fear they felt on these occasions. The second part of their interim period in contrast was most enjoyable, as their father was given custody of the family and they all lived under one roof with their future step-mother and grandparents. 'It was a release from the pressures and fights'.

'My brother had struggled hard to be man of the house whilst we lived with Mum on her own, then he lost his position. His responsibilities were all taken from him. It was worse for him than for me because my step-father was jealous of him.'

Brian remembers his step-father as 'great fun'. Until the age of seven he had lived with his mother and grandmother — 'A dreadful combination for a small boy' he says.

Pat experienced much shuttling to and fro between the separated parents after their break, two days here, four weeks there, time at Gran's etc. She spoke of her deplorable behaviour during that time, particularly towards her own mother, including foul language and nasty letters. Now happily married, she speaks of 'the deep need these children have to be cared for all the time, comforted in the knowledge that they aren't alone in their misery, frustration and anger'.

'I was passed around from one relative to another like a parcel'. Of the interim period, Jacky says: 'It was too short; there wasn't enough time to accustom myself. We were dumped here.'

'During the four years which had elapsed since the death of my mother I had begun to imagine myself taking her place, in my father's affections as well as in the home. This young woman father was introducing me to was obviously a threat, not only to my aspirations as a substitute for my mother, but also as a possible means of ousting me from his affections altogether.'

Loss and grief

Dave's mother died when he was eleven and he was extremely upset about it. When his father remarried, even though he did so only after testing out his children's opinions and giving them a good period to think it all over, things did not work out: 'The first week was OK but then all us kids got stroppy. I wouldn't accept that she was taking my real Mum's place. We didn't feel we could tell her all the things you like to tell your Mum rather than your Dad. We gave her a bad time. We was little gits.' The children all left home as soon as they could. 'If I had had the knowledge I have now [at nineteen], I'd not have been that bad. I thought she was trying to take Mum's place but she wasn't, she was only trying to help.'

'He was an intruder, taking my Mum. I felt a terrible loneliness and was hurt that I could not be part of things.'

When Caroline's father left home, she turned to her boyfriend and became heavily involved with him. After her father's remarriage, she was 'cut up and upset' about hardly ever seeing him. 'I missed my father a lot and jumped into another relationship with another boyfriend. I felt rejected by my father. Now I feel I'm missing out, I regret something. He left and I tried to replace him with other relationships too quickly'.

'I feel rejected and sorry for myself at times. I've never really had a mother'. John's parents split up when he was three and he has never got on well with his step-mother. He is longing for a close relationship with a girl and, at nineteen, says 'I reckon I am sticking out for a *real* relationship you know, not just any old gal'. His mother shows no interest in him at all. She now has a son by her second marriage whom John would dearly like to see a lot of 'as a brother and relative' but he is not allowed to go near.

After her father remarried, Jacky became very resentful and difficult to handle. 'I don't think I ever became close to my father after that, it phased out slowly and I wanted to be so close to Dad. I was frightened too at the way mother had become so *young*; she turned to drink, crashed cars etc. I was very upset and got very little sleep when at her house. I would wake up in a cold sweat wondering was mum in and was she OK.'

'It's very frightening, going through this divorce and remarriage. I don't feel fully loved here at heart, nor even at Mum's.'

'I missed our childhood home. You're told nothing will change when there is a divorce and so on, you won't be loved any less etc. but this just is not so.'

'When divorcees remarry, they tend to leave their children behind; they are on cloud nine but the kids are still coping. They find it difficult to follow on. The parents should slow down and wait for us to catch up.'

Susan had great difficulty when it came to a question of which parent she should live with after they split up. 'There was always a bad feeling with me because I had rejected my mother. It was heavy on my conscience. I was pro-father at the time of his wedding and didn't see Mother. The relationship with my mother went downhill from that time and never picked up again. Was it my fault I wonder? Can you have that sort of fault at sixteen? I *did* have a very good relationship with her before the break.'

4.

LOYALTIES AND JEALOUSIES

These two words occurred so frequently during the course of my discussions with other members of step-families that they warrant a chapter of their own. Adults can handle a family situation much better if they take the trouble to understand what the child is feeling so we shall look at the subject firstly through the eyes of the child and secondly through those of the parent.

Mixed Loyalties

When a child's parents separate and divorce he is placed, after due consideration by the authorities, into the custody of one of them. He may be interviewed by someone such as a probation officer if he is old enough so that his preference for either parent can be taken into consideration, or he may simply be given to the parent who has proved to be the best for the child under the circumstances. Either way, the child can be left feeling very mixed up about who is his 'real' parent — the absent one or the new step-parent. He can feel that he is 'betraying' his natural parent by transferring his affections to the new step-parent. He might feel that he loves the absent parent much more than the parent who has been granted custody. In other words the child can be pulled many different ways at once when the family re-forms, and the question of where to place his loyalties can loom largely, even at a tender age.

What is needed then, is a good understanding of how your child feels on the subject of the absent parent, which is not always achieved without a good deal of pain, because the child is not yet mature enough to cope with all these 'adult' questions and peculiar feelings of loyalty. Once you know basically how he feels you have some grounds for making your own adjustments; you will know why he behaves in a certain manner, which hitherto you might have simply condemned or ignored. Be aware of his thoughts and feelings and you are half-way towards doing something practical to resolve any awkward situations which may arise.

Half-brothers and Sisters

We come now to jealousy and the resentment it produces. Often in a step-marriage the two partners decide they would like children 'of their own', for want of a better phrase, usually with the idea in mind that a 'mutual' baby would be a bond with which to seal the marriage.

Sometimes the proud parents lavish so much attention on the new arrival that the step-children begin to feel a coldness in their direction. They feel somewhat slighted or second best and this results in jealousy of the baby whose arrival has produced this change. I can have sympathy with both sides — naturally, the parents are as proud as can be of their offspring and indeed it can be a special symbol for them, a binding, sealing element to their union. Perhaps they go overboard a little in their attention and this is all it needs for the other children to feel twinges of envy, especially if they have already suffered rejection or loss during the period prior to the remarriage.

Sally, a step-child with whom I have talked at length about her experiences, remembers being thrilled at the prospect of a baby in the family. She and her sister were simply dying to be little mothers and help take care of it, but what happened instead was quite different. Her step-father, with whom she already had a stormy relationship, would not allow the girls to handle the baby and discouraged them from going anywhere near it in case 'his own' child should be in any way influenced by the little girls' bad behaviour. More friction therefore resulted and eventually jealousy and resentment followed. Had he considered for a moment how badly the two girls needed to love and handle the baby, he would have seen what an improvement could have been made in relationships all round. The girls might have begun to love their step-father more through sharing their love for the baby and the new arrival could have been a saving factor in a quickly disintegrating family relationship.

Consider carefully then, your existing children's feelings concerning a new baby. Involve them from the very beginning in preparations for the event, such as shopping for baby clothes. Then after the new arrival give them a share in looking after the baby; let them feel needed at this time in particular and you will soon find that a new baby adds an extra dimension to your step-family rather than dividing it.

Us and Them

Under this heading I want to consider how one set of children feels when living under the same roof as another set, both from different parents, one of whom is present and one absent. I make it sound complicated deliberately for it is as far as the children involved are concerned.

As adults, you may think you have taken on quite a task under these circumstances, but have you really looked at it from the children's point of view? They are having to adapt and cope just as much as you are, but are nowhere near as mature and experienced. They have to struggle with their own personal problems of growing up as well as all the extra conditions imposed on them by your marriage and the uniting of two families. It is only natural that the two sets of offspring will be quick to perceive any differences, real or imagined, in the way in which they are treated by you and your partner. The tiniest things can be enlarged in the mind of an insecure child until they reach epic proportions, especially when he or she is on the look-out for 'different' treatment in any case. Having one less roast potato than the others can be significant to a child who already feels perhaps that he/she isn't loved as much as the other children in the step-family.

When you notice signs of jealousy among your two sets of children ask yourselves whether you are guilty of any favouritism; whether you have distributed anything unequally, be it food, love, attention or whatever. Better still, if you can't recall any particular incidents, find a suitable moment to ask the child concerned what is causing the trouble. It is much better to bring problems into the open than to allow resentment to smoulder in the hope that it is a passing phase.

Age Differences

When a parent remarries and chooses someone only a little older than his or her own family, all kinds of jealous feelings can arise, some of them very difficult to avoid. In particular when a father takes a very young second wife, his daughter can be very jealous. She has already suffered the loss of her mother one way or another and to have a step-mother who could well be her own big sister creates all manner of mixed feelings inside the girl. She probably feels there is something indecent or improper in her father's new relationship; she will feel jealous of all the attention this young woman receives; she might feel that her natural mother is being dishonoured or forgotten. She will also be of an age herself where she has to cope with a lot of new feelings and emotions, which does not help. A son also can be embarrassed by his father's choice if she appears a far more suitable match for himself than his Dad.

There are two main ways in which parents of widely differing ages can help overcome these natural consequences. First, they can be more tactful in their relationship in front of the family. It will help if father stops showing his love for his new wife quite so blatantly and reserves it for more private moments. Secondly, he could take his daughter aside quietly at a suitable moment and try to explain that he loves both wife and daughter deeply, but each in a different way and in no sense could the one ever think that she was in competition with the other because there is no comparison between them.

A very common problem arising from a narrow age gap involves authority. How can teenagers look upon their father's new wife as 'mother' when she is only in her twenties? And conversely, how can the new mother carry an air of authority about her and expect these young people to respect her wishes?

The answer to the first question is that if it is utterly impossible to assume a mother/child relationship, the best thing to do is to look upon yourself as a very good friend and earn your respect from that angle, for without respect for your position as their father's wife, the step-relationship is going to founder. It's no good forcing an attitude from the children, better to have a healthy respect than a false relationship in name only. You can become their friend and adviser very quickly by being sympathetic to their problems, being a good listener and a ready helper. Once the respect has been gained and you cease trying to enforce the

'Do as I say' command, you will find that you no longer need to strive for authority since your relationship will have changed and there will not be such a need for you to use it. Your 'public relations officer', the children's father, can also be employed on these occasions; let him be aware of your difficulties and he can take it tactfully from there, using the authority he has had from the beginning.

The Absent Parent

'You can't have your cake and eat it'. This is a fitting remark if you are a parent who has remarried and you have left your family in the care of your former partner. Naturally you will still feel the family bond, the blood relationship, however happy your new family life appears to be and you might somehow feel that you have rejected or deserted them. To make amends for this you can soon find yourself paying more attention to your former family than is wise under your new circumstances. Your new family will naturally be very sensitive on this issue as they will feel you care more about the past then the present, which is not a good start to a fresh way of life.

If you have had to leave your former partner and family you cannot rightly expect to intrude on their lives as and when you fancy. I recently met a step-father who is trying hard to establish a good relationship with his step-children and is continually hampered by the fact that their real father keeps phoning at all hours to chat to them. The step-family is not given a moment's peace in which to work out its relationships. An extreme example of unwise interference occurred within the same family only recently. The eldest child incurred a fine for some misdemeanour, which the step-father expected him to pay to teach him a painful lesson. A cheque for the whole amount came through the post from the natural father, to his son's delight, and ruined all the careful training which the step-father had been giving. Feelings of love and loyalty are good in themselves, but when they occur within this situation they have to be very carefully controlled indeed. More will be said on this theme of interference later, as it can appear in various guises.

Closely connected to the question of loyalty to a previous family is the subject of maintenance payments. Since the law is in a state of flux on this theme, I do not propose to say too much about it except to ask a question of the new wife. How do you feel about seeing a regular sum of money flowing out of your bank account and into that of your husband's ex-partner? You should have already discussed the point before you married, but now that it is actually happening and perhaps even some of your own hard-earned contribution to the family coffers is disappearing, how does it feel? Naturally your first feelings will be something akin to resentment. Consider instead how your husband must be feeling — he can't enjoy playing his role of dual provider surely and, unless there is plenty of money around, he must be feeling the strain. He is doing something he is legally required to do, so do not be too quick to accuse him of giving too much attention to his former family. Be sympathetic and patient, don't nag and chide as this can only make the situation worse, and never let your husband feel like a turncoat in his new family. When you come up against a situation like this which you are powerless to alter, you might just as well put it right out of your mind and wait for things to change for the better in due course. Everyone knows that love is far more important than money so concentrate on the love in your new marriage and blot out those feelings of resentment or jealousy.

'You Don't Care About Us Anymore'

When you begin your second marriage it is very easy to be in such a state of marital bliss or to concentrate so hard on getting your own relationship right this time, that you tend to forget how the children might be feeling. How do you think they feel when mother or father part from their other parent and take a new partner, furthermore expecting them to carry on as usual as if this were a normal situation?

Sally is a step-child, now grown up and happily married, who told me of her stormy relationship with her step-father who adored her mother to the exclusion of the children. He put her first in his order of loyalties and made this quite plain to the two girls in the step-family. They became bitter and resentful which led to the bad behaviour which he always picked on during arguments. On one occasion Sally had cycled to a neighbouring village for some reason and had left her bike against a hedge. When she returned it was gone, stolen, and she had to phone home for a lift. Her step-father was livid as he was just on the point of taking her mother out to dinner, a special 'twosome' occasion, and he never really forgave Sally for ruining this outing, powerless though she was to alter the situation. This event is still imprinted on her mind; she was made to feel she was getting in the way of her parents' relationship.

This is indeed a common problem among step-families but need never reach the pitch which Sally reports if you go about things sensibly. Organize your family life so that you and your partner do have some time alone together, but make sure that you also give up plenty of time to family events. Friends and baby-sitters can help if your family is very young, and if they are older you can organize for them to be doing their own thing that evening also. If you want to entertain friends at home as a couple rather than a family, tell the children so and ask them if they wouldn't mind either arranging to go out themselves, or doing something in their own rooms for one evening. This is no great hardship for them and it leaves you free to feel like a newly-married couple, which I think is important. If your entertainment involves a meal, why not let the children help prepare some of it if they are interested, or at least make sure they have their own portion to try if it is something special. All these little touches will indicate that you aren't sweeping them out of your way but that you want them to understand how important it is to you to be just husband and wife now and then instead of parents. I have met several couples who told me they simply never went out together without 'hangers-on' and I find it difficult to have sympathy for them because with a little firmness and tact these events can be organized and enjoyed as a necessary part of marriage.

'Hey, What About Me?'

This was literally the cry of George, a step-father who married a woman with four children. He called them a 'close fivesome' and often felt that his wife Sue was lavishing too much attention on them when he was feeling the need of a share himself. Sue, who had been managing the children on her own for some years, felt guilty that she had somehow put them in this situation and tended to divide her loyalties somewhat unevenly between husband and children when they all joined up together. George was made to feel an outsider, so strong and obvious was the bond between the fivesome, even though he and Sue were also firmly attached to each other, and his advice after several years of step-parenting is 'Never neglect your new partner in favour of your children'.

The lesson to learn from these two different examples must surely be to balance our loyalties and affections, to be sensitive to both parties' needs and demands and to show them both that you care how they feel. The fact that George is a sensible mature character has kept his step-family going; he has weathered the experience of feeling he is playing second fiddle to the children and has also communicated with his wife on the matter, so that she is now more aware of what was happening. They continue to live happily together because of his tolerance and love, whereas Sally's family has now split up because of the step-father's intolerance and blindness to his step-children's feelings; Sally still feels resentment, years later, as an adult herself.

Integrating the Family

The secret of success in what I will call the 'double' step-marriage lies with the parents and how they have brought up their separate broods. A lot also depends on the age groups involved. If you have both brought babies or toddlers along with you, you should find that they will soon accept each other, since their memories are short and they have no preconceived ideas about life.

If there is one young group of children and one older group it can often happen quite naturally that the older ones will 'mother' or 'father' the others, so if this sounds like your situation try to encourage this relationship. Give the older ones jobs and responsibilities with regard to the younger ones so that not only do they quickly learn to love them as normal little brothers and sisters, but also feel that they have a great part to play within the family. Apart from all this, of course, your own duties can be relieved slightly at a time when you might be feeling the need for extra time to yourselves.

When the children are all in the older age bracket, this is the most difficult step-family to handle. Give and take, tolerance, patience, sensitivity and endless supplies of love are the ingredients needed for one of these mixtures.

Jealousy, as we expected, will be a problem as far as the children are concerned, but what about your own reactions? Often I hear step-parents complain bitterly about how unfairly their partner treats the two sets of children, favouring their own and discriminating against their step-children. Occasionally a parent bends over backwards not to do this, resulting in an obvious favouring of the others, to the amazement of their own! When these situations arise it is best to get all the family together under some pretext, possibly at a meal-time, and put it to them quite plainly that all of you are going to have to work hard at rubbing along together, parents included.

In a large family group there are a number of practical steps you can take to ease the situation. Everyone needs privacy at times so try to organize your available space with this in mind. Weigh up the natures of your children before allotting bedrooms and try not to segregate the two sets of children too obviously. A room for family activities is also a good idea if you are lucky enough to have the space, thus allowing another quieter room for you two parents but always avoid saying 'this is yours, this is ours'; that kind of approach would never work.

Mutual respect must be encouraged and taught among the children, as with any normal family. Just because some of the hobbies or activities of one group differ widely from those of another, it doesn't mean that the two cannot live together harmoniously. Talk to them about this aspect, either separately or all together, and remember to set them a good example, for you can be sure you will be under scrutiny.

Compromise is a key word in the mixed step-family. Really work hard to find a solution to problems which will be acceptable to both sets of children and look on yourselves as liaison officers during those first few months; act as go-betweens until the children are ready to handle their own differences then quietly withdraw and leave them to it.

Delegate jobs in a large household so that everyone feels they are contributing to the family happiness and so that you parents are not so overwhelmed by extra work that you don't have time to enjoy family life.

If you found it difficult to get to know your future step-children before your marriage, now is the time to remedy the situation. The more you know about their interests, their friends, their activities (without prying of course), the better you will understand how they 'tick', which will stand you in very good stead when it comes to confrontations, strange behaviour, etc. This is an excellent time because it means you will be giving them plenty of attention just when they might otherwise be feeling anything but at ease with the new situation.

If you have brought up your offspring to have consideration for others you will be well on the road to success; if this is lacking (as in a case I know where the step-daughters stood by and watched their new mother do all the housework completely by herself) this must be one of the first things the natural parent should get to grips with. In this particular case the step-mother temporarily left the home with her three children to show the others how it felt to do all the chores themselves. They soon found out but too late; it was only when the children had begun to drift off to college and jobs that the situation began to ease, in spite of the two parents trying their hardest to make the family relationship a success.

You must aim then as parents, to forget the differences between your own children and the step-children and fuse the two together. Naturally, your instinct is to be loyal to your own children and stick up for them when they are criticized (for after all, this criticism really reflects on yourself as teacher of the children) but if you are hoping to teach all the children the meaning of give and take, respect etc., you as parent have to set the pattern. Talk to your partner about all this whenever you feel that two separate camps are forming within the household and you will find that the more open you are about it, the easier it will be to handle.

Case Histories

'I now have to decide whose wing I am under as there are two totally different points of view, two camps. Which should I give my allegiance to?'

Jacky gained two step-brothers when her father remarried. 'We were all treated equally, in fact Dad gave more pocket money to them than me because they were older. I thought "I'm his real daughter and I am getting less" — I couldn't handle that one. I wanted more love and attention from Dad but see now that he had to try to be fair to his step-sons.'

'Those two [step-brother and sister] had money, probably from their father, and a bit of resentment crept in; they seemed to have had more of everything like foreign travel and motor bikes, go-karts, etc. My brother would have loved a go-kart.'

'Who should I ask money from? Not from Dad because he didn't have much. Not from Mum because it wouldn't be right to spend it whilst living with Dad.'

'With Mother it's "husband first" and therefore the children came second and felt it to be so too. I couldn't decide who to live with. I used to have a fit and make excuses about living with either side.'

'When my step-sister was twenty-one there was a huge celebration for her, with all the works; when I was twenty-one there were just a few people round. When my step-sister married there were coaches, crossed swords at the church door, etc. My wife and I on our wedding day were refused the use of a room in the house and had to make do with village hall chairs and so on.'

'When my step-sister was born, I had to move away at twelve years old to live with my grandmother again, as there wasn't enough room in the house. Baby-sitting duties were always forced on me, however.'

Pat's step-father's two children only stayed one week in the home while she was living there, but that was enough. 'The tension was enormous. I thought "what right have they to run wild in my home?" — their behaviour was particularly wild at that time. I blew up and said to Jack (my step-father) "This isn't fair, I'm getting treated rotten in my own home." I used foul language and finally went to sulk in the back yard.'

'I felt rejected by my father. He was more concerned about his new wife.'

John is tired of the embarrassment his step-mother causes him and his friends. 'She gets at me in front of everyone; even my friends come in for some stick as well. My step-sister can have friends round and I can't. I didn't even get invited to the party they gave for my step-sister when she was eighteen. It was nearly a fiasco as a result of all the taking of sides over that by the relations.'

About her mother's new baby by her step-father, Caroline says 'I love him and he loves me. I feel a bit jealous of Father's new children, however, because I don't see them very often and they have a nice life over there.' They live abroad.

'There might be conflict with Mum's new baby and me and my step-father later when he grows up — he might feel a divided loyalty.' Caroline has never got on well with her step-father, which prompted her to make this remark.

'We get no financial support from Dad and our little half-brother is favoured. We come second.' Stuart and his sister live with their mother and step-father now and he forsees possible arguments in the future over this. 'But I don't mind anything so long as Dad cares about us.'

Caroline's father married a young girl only two years older than herself. 'It makes me uncomfortable and she uses their children to get at me. I hope to be friends one day. I didn't believe she was sincere when she invited me to the wedding.'

'I was quite surprised to be taken by Father when I was fourteen to meet a woman only ten years older than myself. I was very jealous at the time; this very attractive young woman was obviously a threat, a possible means of ousting me from Father's affections altogether. On my father's return to sea, my step-mother and I began our journey into a relationship in the real sense.' (Paula had had initial difficulties accepting a very young step-mother and then had been revolted and appalled to hear of a baby on the way.)

'She was obviously unsure of how to deal with me and her position in the house and kept seeking reassurance. We quickly established a relationship similar to that of sisters — we were both only children at it happened — which has continued to develop. We shared the difficulties of the care of the baby, not an easy child in its first year. It brought us closer together in Father's absence.

'We did experience a few difficulties when she tried to lay down the law about the hours I kept and the company. I simply walked out on these occasions, but feared my father's wrath when he should hear of it from her.

'I think if there is a relatively small age difference it is vital that the step-parent should be an ally to the child in some respect. The authoritarian image can be maintained by the existing parent, provided it is there in the first place.'

5.

PARENT, EX-PARENT, STEP-PARENT

You will, I hope, already have discussed your plans for accommodating whatever access agreement has been reached, if there has been a divorce before your remarriage. Now that it is time to organize these meetings you will find that there are ways and means of going about it in order to cause the least hurt to any involved party. As I have stated earlier, Peter Rowland's book, *Saturday Parent,* gives excellent advice on the subject of access.

Usually, neither party of adults finds the access visits easy to cope with, to say nothing of the children themselves. I think it might help if we look at the problem from these separate angles and bear in mind that these meetings are basically for the *child's* benefit, not one's own.

The Custodial Parent
How often have I heard a step-parent complain that there will never be a chance to get on with the business of living with and loving someone else's children if there is continual interruption and upheaval caused by visits, calls and letters from the 'ex-parent'? The custodial parent is caught in the cross-fire and has to try and pacify the step-parent but neither does he/she exactly relish these visits and intrusions by his/her ex-partner on his/her new family life Unpleasant memories, embarrassment and pain are all part of the scene, just when things ought to be starting afresh and it seems that there will be no end to the past.

My advice is to accept the situation as it stands and proceed to make the very best of it, with your child's interests at heart. If you feel hurt, jealous and depressed every time your child or step-child is whisked away for the day or weekend by the 'access parent', it's no good sitting about moping. Organize a treat for yourself; have a new hair-do and don't worry about the expense; go on a shopping spree, visit somewhere; in other words make something of that day for yourself so that when your child or step-child returns, you can both have something to tell each other about the day's events.

If you hate to have any contact at all with the access parent try to arrange things in such a way that you need not meet; for instance, the child could be collected from the home of a mutual and sympathetic relative.

Understand your child's view of things. Young children in particular live for the present and will accept whatever good things are in store for them, regardless of where they come from. You will find it extremely hard, for instance, to see your child return home clutching that new radio which he has begged from you for weeks but which you couldn't afford or thought he shouldn't have just yet. He doesn't know how hurt you feel nor why you are angry that your authority has been undermined. The only way to stop such occurrences as these is to have a ready line of communication with the other parent and use it when necessary, which is not always easy to do. Some acquaintances of mine who have a 'double' step-family have good relationships all round. Lucy's ex-husband is very happy to sort out problems involving his girls who are in her care — he advises by phone or acts on decisions but never arrives on the doorstep or forces himself upon the family. When the girls go to their 'other' home for a week, Lucy's present husband gladly takes them and has a chat at the other end of the journey. Lucy's daughter Chris amazes her friends when she mentions that her Mum and her step-mother both talk together and are friendly, though never imposing on each other. This rather proves that the common concept of the real and step-parent relationship is one of animosity and hate. Lucy's family situation is regrettably the exception rather than the norm, but I use the example to illustrate how things can be made easier all round by accepting access as a legal right and secondly organizing it in a sensible and civilized manner whilst still maintaining harmonious relationships at home.

The Non-custodial Parent

The hardest thing for the non-custodial parent to swallow is the fact that he/she now has the minor role to play in the upbringing of his/her own child. That child is entrusted partly into the hands of a complete stranger. How can you be sure that the person knows and loves your child well enough to do the job properly; does that person have the right qualities to pass on to your child? Doubts and fears must make life miserable at times.

The access parent is frequently accused of using bribery to gain affection and I have an example of this among my collected case histories. A teenaged boy was living quite happily with his mother after her divorce until his father decided he wanted more than just the occasional visit. He literally bought his son's affection and loyalty with offers of lots of money to spend and a luxurious life abroad with a glamorous young step-mother and himself. At such an impressionable age the boy could not say no and left his mother for the new life. Eventually the boy returned after seeing how hollow and unreal was the promised way of living but not until much damage had been done to relationships all round. This is an extreme example but it shows the real dangers of trying to gain affection by corrupt means.

It is easy to understand why the access parent often gives in to bribery or takes part in the 'Father Christmas' syndrome, when gifts are constantly showered upon the child. The parent feels he must somehow make up for what has gone wrong with the original marriage; he also feels he must draw attention to his love for the child by making these extravagant gestures when he does get the chance to see him, lest during his absence the child might forget him. He fears too that the new step-parent will draw his child away from him and sometimes is tempted to paint a larger-than-life picture of this person's defects in order to stop the affections going too deep. He feels a resentment that other people might get along well with his child when it has been judged that he personally is not the right parent for that child to live with and hence is tempted to 'interfere' with the new step-family. This is indeed a black picture I have painted and of course it is not true of every access parent but it is designed to show the traps you might fall into if you are in this situation.

Now let's look at some positive things you can do to better your situation. First, make sure that you stick to the provisions made for your access since they will have been carefully worked out already. Be punctual when meeting your child and always give advance warning if you can't make an appointment or need to alter an arrangement. Remember that you don't have to have a treat in store; your child ought to be happy just to be sharing some sort of activity with you, however mundane.

At this point I am prompted to mention a friend I spoke to recently who is a 'Saturday parent' himself. He is intelligent and far-sighted and when he heard that his daughter was boasting to her friends that she would be doing something 'special' each Saturday with her Dad, he decided to test whether it was the 'something special' or the 'being with Dad' that she enjoyed. He also realized how hard it would be on his ex-wife (whom, incidentally, he hated seeing each time he called for his daughter), to compete with these Saturday events during the rest of the week. Accordingly he organised nothing for the following Saturday and when his daughter looked at him expectantly, calmly announced that they were going shopping at Sainsbury's. She groaned and made a face but gladly tagged along with Dad and his new wife and spent the rest of the day cycling about the street making friends and generally doing nothing. In other words, this Saturday parent had the nerve to test his daughter's affections and bring her down to earth with a bang. She survived and so did his position in her life.

One important function of the access parent is to be a willing listener but by that I don't mean a listener to tell-tale stories about the child's step-family life (unless, of course, something is really wrong). When a child is growing up it's often easier to talk to someone slightly removed from the close home situation and the former parent can fulfil this function very naturally if he is at all receptive. He can advise but never impose his authority; a wise access parent will always help the child to try to understand the custodial parent's point of view and only when this seems totally unreasonable should the non-custodial parent attempt to interfere personally.

The Child

The child of a step-family needs continuity and stability; the knowledge that certain things will always remain the same. He has already experienced a marital break-up or a bereavement and

PARENT, EX-PARENT, STEP-PARENT

now has to face up to living with one real parent plus a new one and seeing his other real parent occasionally. He will need to know exactly when the visit will take place and will be upset if ever there are last-minute hitches, hence the need for the two parents to keep in communication, however distant.

The child will be assailed by mixed loyalties, not knowing whether he is right to feel happy when with the other parent or whether he is somehow being 'disloyal' to the custodial one. He will most likely be aware of tension and stress in his home when these visits are imminent, sensing it but not fully understanding it, which all adds to his misery and confusion. You as parent must do your utmost to hide your real feelings at this stage lest they influence the child — let him be free to enjoy the different types of company of both of you without fears and inhibitions.

There might even be times when the child refuses to meet the other parent and tries all manner of tricks to persuade you he can't go. On these occasions never actually force him to go; instead, let the access parent know what is going on and ask him if he can think of any reasons why this reaction has set in. Also try asking the child when the moment is right and always show your love and understanding instead of exasperation.

A child whose non-custodial parent has a widely differing lifestyle and standards from those he is used to will no doubt return home and be very awkward to manage at first until he settles back to the accustomed routine. He simply doesn't know which set of standards to adopt when he is continually moving from one parent to another. In this case your best way out as parent is to contact the other one and try to put it to them that it might not be a good idea to let the child suffer this change so frequently.

We have looked now at the bone of contention about access from three viewpoints and can hopefully draw some general conclusions. One thing dominates the whole issue; the child's welfare must be considered paramount. Bearing this in mind therefore, try to forget your own pain and jealousy, your fears, doubts and hurt pride, and concentrate on doing what seems best for the child or children. When behaviour difficulties arise, force yourself to get together with the access parent (even if only on the phone) and discuss any salient points he or she can offer advice upon. Keep open your lines of communication about visits to avoid the anguish and fears a child may feel when no parent turns up at the appointed place. Never impede contact with a former parent by opening letters addressed to the child or refusing to allow a conversation by telephone. In the long run it does not help for when the child eventually becomes aware of these obstacles he is going to lose all confidence in you as custodial parents which will in turn only lead to further complications within your step-family relationships.

Aim to be on reasonable terms with the partner of the access parent. Often this person is far enough removed yet sufficiently involved by marriage to be a great asset as a go-between when unbearable tensions arise between ex-partners. Try not to come out with sweeping statements about the break-up of the first marriage — children are easily impressed and you could colour their view of the absent parent permanently instead of letting them take things at face value until they are old enough to decide for themselves.

What a formidable list of do's and don'ts! Access has always caused bitterness and frustrations in step-families and most likely always will so my advice can only be to keep an eye open for signs of emotional disturbance in your child before and after visits, to have a listening ear at all times and to be sensible enough to forget your differences when necessary and communicate with the other parent on points of mutual benefit.

An Alien In Your Own Home

I have heard this phrase or something akin to it many times during my talks with other step-parents, and can identify with it easily having suffered from that feeling myself during my early experience of step-parenthood. There are, I think, two separate ways in which we step-parents feel sometimes like utter strangers or guests within our families. Firstly there is the fact that we have come from outside to join an existing close family group with its own set of rules and customs which leads naturally to these alien feelings and secondly there is the fact that in many cases we have moved physically into someone else's household full of material and tangible evidence of a former way of living.

Me versus Them

This was my view of taking on a family in my early days as step-parent and I know it is a natural feeling. There they all were, husband and three belligerent boys, all defiantly (so it seemed) sticking close together and hanging on to all their old ways without taking an ounce of notice of anything I felt should be altered. One against four — how unfair after all the trouble I had been taking to try to fit in with them, I used to think, but now how differently I can see things thirteen years later.

I understand now why they remained so close and hung on to familiar patterns of life. Their lives had been seriously disrupted prior to my arrival. How were they to be sure that I was going to be a good mother and care for them in every way that a natural mother would? I know now that I was looking for something of me in the children, hoping that they would somehow reflect a little of my character as soon as I took charge, to make everything 'normal' and nice. How could they and why should they? Their characters were formed already by heredity and upbringing and I had had nothing to do with them until the year before so who was I to think I could barge in and take over just like that? However, this understanding comes with hindsight and most of us who experience these feelings of opposition during the first year or so of our step-marriage are so busy trying to get everything right and appear confident that we probably fall into the trap of overdoing things and are so bossy about our 'takeover' that we fail to consider the deeper feelings of our family.

Step-fathers can experience this alien feeling too, of course. George, previously mentioned in Chapter 4, married his 'close fivesome' as he called it and has never really felt a true part of the family in spite of his tolerance and intelligent handling of the situation. Maybe he never will. The family had managed well together for a number of years prior to the remarriage so it is understandable that the children felt no need of a father since they did not even have any communication with their natural father.

The best solution which I can offer to the impasse which occurs when you feel you cannot 'get through' to your new family in spite of all your efforts is to call upon your public relations officer — your husband or wife. Who better to handle a delicate family situation than the person who knows and loves both parties concerned? Tell them your difficulties and leave it to them to do some diplomatic talking, being careful however, not to let it appear to the children that you can't handle things on your own. If the children are old enough to understand I think it can often be a good thing to lower your pride and admit to them that you have taken on a difficult task and will need all the help they can give. Children appreciate adult confidences and it could well work wonders if they realize that they are important and have a responsibility towards helping you in your new job.

Another person's home

Little needs to be said about the difficulties created when you move into your partner's home, whether you move in as step-parent or whether you go with your family. All who have experienced this feeling of being a stranger among someone else's furniture and fittings know just how bitter, upset and jealous you can become in spite of yourself.

We have already discussed in Chapter 2 the pros and cons of moving from your existing home upon your remarriage but here we consider the plain facts which exist when you have no choice but to start off your new life in someone else's home. Extreme cases have come to my notice where photographs of the former partner who has died have remained firmly in view in spite of gentle hints by the new partner to the effect that they find this unsettling. Someone else's taste is evident throughout the house in the choice of furniture, wallpaper, cushions or whatever and if you find you simply cannot abide it, then you must tell your partner so; nothing is gained by remaining heroically silent because your partner is so accustomed to his or her home that he or she will probably never guess the cause of your discomfort. Whether you can manage to redecorate or buy new furniture is a matter of personal finances, but something which you can do gradually is to add your own personal touches here and there to the home. I say 'gradually' because if the family has lived there for some time, the members will become very hurt and upset if you start altering all things dear and familiar to them as soon as you arrive. Give and take will have to be employed and you will have to keep reminding yourself that eventually some of those dreadful plates will break and *you* can choose new ones; the carpet will wear out, the wallpaper will need a change and gradually you can make your own mark around the home.

One final remark from me about these feelings of alienation

is that you must never give up when you know that you are right on a point. You will always remain an alien or outsider if you always give in and let the family go its usual old way. Work hard at gaining their respect and their love will follow but it will take time. This will be a testing point for your new role and as such must be taken very seriously by you; examine what you are doing and saying within the family and ask yourself now and then if you are doing it the best way or if you could use more tact and patience. Looking back I can see any number of wrong moves which I made; if you can bear all this in mind at the beginning of your new family life you can most likely save everyone a great deal of friction and unnecessary pain.

Case Histories

Access

'Our visits to Dad were well organized and regular but after seeing him I then had to go back home for the rest of the week and would have to get all my feelings back into perspective again only to be disrupted once more as the following weekend loomed.'

'It used to be half and half — one part of the school holidays with Mum and the other with Dad. Now I have to decide where to stay. I don't want to be apart from my brother; since the split-up he started to care and love me in his own way.

'There is a big clash now with my mother and myself over fashion, make-up, etc. I find it painful to see my mother "competing" with me. All this "rivalling" after the split was to gain my love and support as her daughter and maybe to persuade me to choose to live with her.'

Mike has seen his mother only rarely over the last twelve years of living away from the area with his father and step-mother. When talking of visiting, he would say 'I'm reluctant to go over old territory by visiting her. I'm worried about what I might feel, I suppose. I don't want to have to face that anymore.'

Letters for him and his brother did arrive during their first year away but 'I didn't answer, I felt no interest.'

Mike and his brothers visited their mother very recently after not seeing her for about six years, so it was interesting to hear how he had felt. 'It was difficult. It's difficult for me anyway to talk to people, but it was made worse by the fact that I hadn't seen her for a long time. I didn't find a lot to say, there was no common ground. Its odd;

not an explainable feeling to tell others about. Its not a pain, just a divided sort of feeling.'

Rosemary and her younger brother have a good access arrangement with their father, now remarried. 'At first Father came to us for a few hours — this was done deliberately for Stuart, who was only two, to get to know a father. He built up those visits gradually until we both spent whole weekends with him and his new wife. 'We liked her and she used to send flowers back with us from the garden for Mum. When I asked her why, she would say "If she's like you two, she deserves them".'

Rosemary feels sure her father is hurt and not happy about his children being absent from his household. 'When he went on so much about how we must use his surname (we had adopted our stepfather's), I used to say to him gently "We still include you, you're not abolished," etc.'

Martin rarely saw his mother, who never tried to see him or his brothers. When he did visit her, 'it was not a pleasant visit, she had changed'.

'I'm not interested in seeing her, she has become a third party, separate. On my last visit there was still an odd strange feeling; I wanted to cringe away in spite of wanting to pay my respects.'

About the letters which arrived during the first year away he says 'I had no feeling or enthusiasm, no incentive to write'.

Chris stayed with her father every other weekend and visits ran smoothly. However, she does comment 'I felt at the time that it wasn't enough, because there were lots of treats and presents and so on. I would have liked to have lived with him then; I was young and impressionable and fell for that treatment.'

'The only interference from Mum after we came to live here with Dad was in connection with my little sister. She was a 'problem child' and I was always getting advice from Mum on how to sort her and Dad out.'

When it comes to 'family occasions' June says a letter will arrive to the effect that 'If your father is there, I won't be'.

Sweeping clean
There were a number of comments about the 'sweeping clean' tactics of newly arrived step-mothers into the children's own homes:

'I'm not having anyone coming into *my* house.' This was what Jacky thought as soon as she heard the news of a step-mother from her father.

'When I heard she was going to take over the household and "mould it into shape", my anger, my God! I smashed windows and Dad was furious. If they hadn't made those changes so quickly it might have been better.' She refers to a complete redecoration of the home upon her step-mother's arrival.

'I was very angry and upset; alienated, turned out of my childhood home, it had been taken over. There were lots of immediate changes, stricter rules.'

Alan and his mother moved in with his new step-father and family. Since this is his mother's third marriage, Alan has 'learnt to take a long cool look at things'.

'I'm aware that in coming into this home I must try not to tread on anyone's toes. This is *their* home. Mother made too many dramatic changes in the home for Tim and his sister. Everything was made new. If she had done it more slowly they could have accepted it more. Their own mother was turfed out.'

An alien in one's own home

Brian's father had died a wartime hero and he, Brian, feels his step-father always felt intimidated by this and therefore not quite at ease in the home. Although a move was made from the family home upon his mother's remarriage, 'there was always an aura of Father around, the house was like a military museum; Father's things were still around'. To explain this fact, Brian says 'Remember that Mother had never fallen out of love with Father, he had simply died.'

'I remember occasions in the early days, and it still happens, when we three and Dad would all be reminiscing about some affair which happened before the break-up and my step-mother would get a distant, 'out-of-it' look on her face until we realized that maybe she was feeling a bit hurt by it all. We never intended to do that to her.'

6.

RELATIVES AND FRIENDS

Outside your immediate step-family group there remains a host of other people including grandparents, other relatives, neighbours and friends, with whom it is advisable to keep good relationships, especially where they existed prior to your reformation as a new family. There are, I think, two main reasons for the apparent suspicion or caution which you as step-parent often sense on the part of these people. First, they probably have the 'wicked step-parent' myth firmly imprinted on their minds, especially if they are of the older generation, as yet unused to the modern instability of marriage and somewhat horrified to see this happening within *their* family. Secondly, they will remember the family and its way of life before you were part of it, and are bound to notice changes and differences, especially if they are on the look-out for them.

Your first move when you sense criticism is to ask yourself whether it is valid. Are you doing something wrong, violating some sacred family tradition for instance? Discuss this with your partner or even be bold enough to ask one of the critics how you are causing offence and explain that you wish to do something about it. If the criticisms are unfounded, these people will be put on the spot by your direct confrontation and might think more positively in future. If there is something of which you were unaware, that is causing discord within the extended family, or 'anti' feelings about you among friends and neighbours, then it is best to swallow your pride and set about improving the situation. Retaining good relationships all round is well worth it even if it means sacrificing a little of yourself in the process because in the long run it benefits your young family to feel that nothing has changed too drastically in spite of their acquiring a new parent. They have already suffered the loss of one parent either by death or divorce and further unnecessary loss of familiar people can only undermine their confidence.

When you find there is no basis for criticism, stand your ground and prove everyone wrong. Show by your determined efforts towards family unity and happiness that you know what you are aiming for and are prepared to risk unpopularity to achieve it. Your partner can help a great deal by pointing out all the good things you as step-parent are doing and have so far achieved; he or she can encourage the critics to overlook the petty differences that seem to engage their attention, point out the long-term goals ahead and also highlight the difficulties and stress already existing for you which are not helped by their interference.

If all fails on the diplomatic front remind yourself that you married the person you love, not his or her relatives. However, a good attempt at public relations work is recommended if only for the sake of the children.

Gossip from neighbours and acquaintances is best ignored or dealt with by a direct approach. You have little to lose personally by offending such people so confront them with their own words and ask what they mean by them or what business it is of theirs to interfere. Most gossips will be dumbfounded by a direct approach as they are used to a behind-the-back method.

If your children suffer at school from malicious talk, usually picked up by their classmates from their own parents, go directly to the headmaster if you cannot talk to the parents themselves. He is trained to deal with such occurrences and will also speak to the parents on your behalf. Cruelty among children is well known but can be controlled and needs swift action from you once you are aware of it. Children may not like to talk about these problems in front of you, so keep yourself well informed, even if it means asking the class teacher to report to you any incidents of taunting. Often a remark such as 'Where does your real Mum live now?' can trigger off a private misery within your child and unless you keep a receptive ear open, you might be unaware of the problem and hence unable to help.

Grandparents

Grandparents have an important part to play in your step-marriage and family life. They are a generation apart from you and most likely hold strong views concerning marriage break-up and divorce. Furthermore, they will remember the previous family routine of course. You are 'replacing' either their offspring or the partner of their offspring so understandably they cannot help but show a deep concern for what is now happening to their family. This concern can come over as criticism and interference at times and is not always welcome when you are trying hard to make your own impression on your new family. However, children have every right to keep in touch with their grandparents; it is their heritage and furthermore, general stability of family life is so often demonstrated by the solid presence of gran and grandad, approaching their umpteenth year of married life, reliable and consistent in character and still caring very much for the children. Keeping on good terms with grandparents should definitely be your aim.

You will find yourself under scrutiny if you live near enough to be observed frequently, and though grandparents are chiefly (we hope) concerned for the children's welfare this close observation can be very unnerving and annoying for the new parent. As allies grandparents can be invaluable but as enemies they are formidable so keep this in mind as you gradually shape your new family group. The children ought not to be deprived of any stabilizing influences in their lives when they have already experienced serious disruption.

If you sense criticism, turn it to your own advantage — ask the grandparents if they think you are doing something drastically wrong and see what advice they can give on how to remedy things. If they can't come up with anything constructive it might make them realize that it would be best to keep quiet about the difficulties you are having as new parent and to offer help only if there is something positive they can suggest.

Secondly, make them feel wanted and needed as an essential cog in the family wheel. They probably feel like helpless bystanders, watching this second marriage with fear and suspicion, so if you can involve them in some small but significant part of it, they might feel that they haven't yet outlived their usefulness. Let Grandpa do a bit in your garden, or let Grandma do a spot of baby-sitting; there are many small gestures of friendliness you can make as step-parent to show them that you value their concern and want their approval.

Thirdly and finally, always clamp down firmly on interference. If it doesn't come best from you as step-parent, make sure your partner does it. I know of at least one case where a grandmother was allowed to wreck a step-family's chances of success. She had always taken care of her son's young family since his wife died and would not let go of the reins when he remarried. She grew into a tyrant whom her daughter-in-law was too weak to resist and whom her son refused to deal with. The marriage ended in divorce and resulted in the wife becoming totally disillusioned about marriage in general, although she had made a good job of bringing up the children before she left.

General public opinion can condemn your efforts to run a step-family. More than once I have heard the remark 'Oh, its because they've got a step-mother you know, she's not their real mother', when referring to some bad behaviour in children. How unfair this is — in one case I know of, the step-mother had taken on the children at such a tender age that they couldn't possibly have experienced anything but a normal life and their unruly behaviour was simply that exhibited occasionally by all children whatever their background.

Unfortunately, until the general public wakes up and realizes what a terribly old-fashioned and narrow view it is taking (something which will be achieved eventually through the media and social services) we step-parents have to ignore the inferences and carry on the good work!

Case Histories

Rodney's father died before he was born and he gained a step-father at the age of four. 'All contact with father's side of the family was broken when mother remarried. There had been an arrangement for a good school for me via my father's parents, but all this went by the board after the marriage. Nothing was actually discussed, they just ignored that side of the family. There was always unpleasantness against that side, my visits to the grandparents as a child were always made difficult. My grandmother had got used to the idea of looking after me and my mother during those first years and actually resented my step-father a little. I did and still do miss not having had anyone to fall back on and talk to as an older person.'

'Gaining grandparents etc., the extended family, is also a plus, I really like my new grandmother and still see my natural one.'

John feels he has lost his natural mother and her relatives through the marriage break-up, and is not allowed to approach his half-brother (from her next marriage) with a view to claiming him as a close friend and relative. However, he has found extra relatives in his step-sister's parents. 'Gail's step-mum and her dad think a lot of me and I enjoy staying there as I can work with her Dad and get away from home for a break. I go alternate weekends and once I was introduced by her Dad to a friend as 'my half-son'. I felt quite proud! I nearly sent him half a Father's Day card!'

'Initially at school I felt different from my friends when they all said "Gosh, isn't she lucky, she's got four parents," but now I feel its the norm to have a mixed background.'

'My friends at school used to think it was odd, being in a step-family, though I wouldn't have thought anything of it. They would ask silly personal questions.'

Mike said he thought that being in a step-family had affected him when relating to other people though he found this very hard to describe: 'Like almost being second, not inferior, but not entitled to the same kind of . . . — you're the same but not quite as good.' This is what he feels as a young adult and compares himself with friends and their families. 'They have had a more stable background, I think to myself.'

Paula had been in the care of her maternal grandmother after her mother died when she was ten. Her grandmother had always been part of the family home and acted as guardian/housekeeper during her father's long absences at sea.

'My grandmother never mentioned the affair to me at all but obviously felt threatened as to her position when Father married again. In retrospect I see she did everything she could to smooth the passage for the new member of the household, although I'm certain her initial feelings were very resentful.'

When the young wife moved into the home, Paula was very surprised that Grandmother moved out. 'I was openly criticized for expressing my feelings of sadness at her departure on the grounds that I had never appeared to be particularly fond of her before.'

Paula, however, eventually welcomed the way in which she gained relatives after being an only and rather lonely child. 'It has extended the range of my family considerably. I would never have had sisters unless the marriage had taken place. I now realize what this means to me.'

7.

TOGETHERNESS

It cannot be stressed strongly enough how important it is to work towards family unity within the step-family group. In my opinion, many 'first time' families have foundered and fallen apart unnecessarily because they simply didn't realize the value of family harmony. Society is based on the family unit; everything else spreads out from there and without it our structure of society breaks down, it's as simple as that.

I use the words 'work towards' deliberately because the step-family is by definition an unnatural group compared with the 'biological' family connected by heredity. It consists of a number of people thrown together (some of them in at the deep end, no doubt) who have not grown up together knowing each other's little quirks and characteristics, good and bad. These have to be discovered within the step-family whereas the normal family is ahead on this score, having it all inborn. We as step-parents therefore, have to think about some aspects which normal families simply experience without thinking, and a certain amount of organization is necessary to allow for this process.

Time
Time must be created if it is not readily available. In a busy household where both parents consider it essential to work full-time, it is important to delegate a few of the time-consuming jobs and to organize other jobs to your own advantage. Every household runs according to the various activities and work

patterns of its members, so no hard and fast rules can be set down here. However, a few ideas might start you thinking up your own schemes.

Spread mundane jobs around the family. Everyone from a tender age upwards can make a bed, wash the dishes, feed the dog, push the vacuum cleaner around, etc.

Jobs such as the family washing can be done after the young family has gone to bed. Ironing can be kept to an absolute minimum by choosing the right types of clothes and linen. Baking is a creative and interesting job which can well be made into an enjoyable shared activity if you let the family literally have a finger in the pie. Car maintainance can also be treated this way — take your children under the bonnet with you, don't just make them clean the car every weekend.

The working step-mother

Whether or not a step-mother ought to work after taking on all her extra responsibilities has been discussed in Chapter 2. Due to financial considerations, many have no choice in the matter but I would like to stress again how much more valuable time is than money; time to think things out, to listen to other people's problems and to have fun with your family. I met one lady whose household set off under severe financial strain, yet she gave up her job on taking on the family and used her time to run the new home and bring the family together as a unit, eventually adding to it with two more babies. She admits it was hard going but feels very strongly that the basics of family life have to come first, the rest following later when everything is going well. Our own family started off under similar financial pressures with the boys eating vast quantities of food and growing out of clothes rapidly but although we were not comfortable financially, we came to know and appreciate each other through having the time to get together frequently as a family.

The opposite side of the picture is met with only too frequently. Sally, whom I have mentioned already as having a difficult step-father, rarely saw her mother at all since her job began almost the minute Sally came home from school. This job also took up the best part of the weekend, traditionally family time for most people. If her mother had only realized what was resulting from this situation she could have tried to change her hours and the step-family might have begun on an entirely different footing.

Communication
In my family, we believe in coming out with grievances, giving them a public airing and trying to do something about the situation, especially if it is having an effect on the whole family. Communication all round is essential for a good family atmosphere. It is good also for the family to see you and your partner enjoying being together, it gives them a feeling of warmth and security, so long as you also share your affections with your children.

An ideal time to set aside for 'family communication' is evening meal-time. If the family members are hungry they will be only too willing to sit down for half an hour or so and enjoy the meal. Also, this might be the only time of the day when each member of the family can be in the one place at the same time. During this time you can talk about your day's events, be it school or work, you can laugh, tease, tell jokes, discuss problems and argue with each other. All of these things represent communication and the family as a whole will benefit from such occasions. I don't know how many times we as a family have said 'We'll talk about it at tea-time'.

At the other end of the scale comes an acquaintance of mine who battled on with her relationship despite a domineering resident mother-in-law and an insensitive husband. She told me there was no communication whatever within the step-family regarding their problems. The husband turned a blind eye or stuck his head in the sand like an ostrich whenever she begged him to talk about what was going wrong. When she finally arranged for the whole family to be in the same room at the same time to force a frank discussion he swept out as soon as he realized what was happening, saying he flatly refused to talk about it and that was that. She is now a very disillusioned divorcee who will never embark on marriage again.

Team Spirit
If you look on your family as a team and you have as your aim happiness and a reasonable amount of harmony and understanding within the group, you will realize that you all need to pull together in the same direction to achieve the aim. Think

of a rowing team, for instance, with you and your partner as trainer and cox. Each member of the team has to be concerned about the others and though you all might be different in nature you have your own position in the family boat which is best suited to your abilities. If one of the team decides to dip his oar in the water when he should be pulling it out, the whole family rhythm will be upset, hence the need for a few rules.

Most step-parents agree with me on the point of having a 'set of rules' or a few principles to go by. The sooner you make your set of rules clear to the family the better, as you can all then set off together in the direction you wish to go. There are, of course, ways of doing this and ways to avoid. You might run the risk of being disliked, particularly if your 'rules' are quite different from what the family had been used to before you came along, but if you go about it tactfully you should get away with it. Your partner can be the one to introduce these new rules to the family, it doesn't necessarily have to be the lot of the step-parent. Let it also be seen by example that you and your partner intend to abide by these principles.

I have made these rules sound rather Victorian but in reality they need only consist of something like consideration for others, honesty and responsibility within the family. Your own 'rules' will spring to mind easily enough once you start thinking about your own family.

Enjoyment

If you feel that you don't do enough together as a family and that you would all benefit from more joint activities, get to work on the idea with your partner. There is no reason now that you are a family to drop all those things we talked of in the 'getting to know each other' period before marriage.

Maybe your children are just waiting for you to show enough interest in some of their individual activities before they involve you in them. Even if you personally don't like fishing, for instance, you can go along with the rest of the family as picnic-provider and simply be around the same area doing whatever it is you like to do, even if it's only sun-bathing or reading. If the whole family is there it means a lot to the children who might otherwise think you don't care much about their lives. If you can muster up the ability to join in your new family's activities, they will be delighted and secretly quite proud of you, especially if they notice that it isn't exactly your usual kind of entertainment.

I have mentioned four areas for step-parents to consider, the first three combining to bring about the fourth, enjoyment, without much extra effort being involved. Make time for being aware of your family and its different members, make sure you are all able to talk and listen to each other sympathetically, apply a few basic rules for pulling together (setting the example yourself) and the rest should follow naturally. Never confuse family pleasure with love; many step-parents feel that if they cannot instantly love their step-children, the family will founder. This is not so; aim at getting to know your new family as closely as possible first of all as a friend or confidant; the love will eventually follow probably unnoticed by you until some family event triggers off a reaction which makes you aware of it. You can still be an integral part of a happy family even if you feel that you have not achieved the aim you set yourself, natural parental love. A close, trusting relationship can be a wonderful thing in itself — aim towards that and let the rest take its course.

Case Histories

Our own boys have always enjoyed family outings and fun together with us during their growing up period and just love any excuse for a bit of a party or celebration. 'Aren't we having wine?' from our youngest son is always the cue which makes me realize that there is something in the family to celebrate and toast, a success at work or school, a return home by a wandering brother and so on.

Susan is very grateful to her step-mother for the good times she has created for the whole family (two sets of children joined up), in spite of being very busy coping with such a household. 'Since our step-mother has been around we've felt much more mature. She has introduced us to so much, things we had no idea about before. Mother and her new partner never went out together, never had friends in and showed little emotion for each other. Dad and Judy [step-mother] used to go out and about and take any of us with them too, she would involve all of us in things, which was good.'

Stuart enthused about how he had formed a great partnership at bowls with his step-father — 'We won the last match we played together,' then in almost the same breath went on to say 'We go swimming with the other family'. He has aspirations as a chef and his mother lets his experiment on the whole family when he wants to, with mixed results kindly tolerated by all those present.

'You can't force a relationship — we drifted on,' says Caroline with regard to her step-father. 'I have a very close relationship with my father and didn't want another — just a friend was all he might be at best. We had no common ground.'

Tom is extremely good at cricket and has achieved national success recently but says 'I get no encouragement these days. I feel especially hurt that Mum does not show enough interest but I think it might be that she associates it with our family life before this family and would rather forget it.'

'My step-father's interests are not remotely like mine so we don't share anything in that way.'

'My step-father never showed any emotion or communication. Nothing was ever spoken out directly. I never received a personal present or birthday card from him; girlfriends were always unwelcome in the home. I was never considered a person in my own right. There was no support from my mother either, she was a very weak person.'

'He didn't understand my mother's mannerisms which apparently showed up in me [Brian was brought up in a feminine household], and tried to talk to me but gave up the attempt when he found no immediate success, he felt he was intruding. He never did it again which was sad because I needed a father and really wanted to know what was wrong.

'He should have been firm and communicated more. He would talk to me for hours about the universe but never about people.'

'I felt no hate for Jim [step-father], because he wasn't hateable; he would always patiently try to sit and talk to me about my feelings. I could never say thank you to him for anything and feel bad about it now.'

On the whole there was very little favourable comment about family togetherness from the children I spoke to. At best they seemed to be just tolerating everyone and getting on with their own lives whilst their parents did likewise.

8.

JOYS

'Is it all worth while?' is the question most of us ask ourselves or our partner when we are in the thick of family trials and tribulations, seemingly never-ending. We surmount one difficulty with a sigh of relief, only to find yet a further one looming rapidly, a process which appears to renew itself deliberately whenever we sit back with a sigh of contentment. But hopefully you will realize that many of your problems are the common ones encountered in every family situation, not specifically in a stepfamily, and this must bring some small comfort.

However, there are sure to be some problems remaining which you find grow out of proportion and indeed do not become any better even when the children reach their late teens and beyond. Under such circumstances as these the weary step-parent sometimes regrets the day he or she ever agreed to 'marry a family' and, not surprisingly, poses the question 'Is it all worth while?' My answer to this question would be an emphatic yes, though if I were to be caught on a bad day I might be seen to hesitate.

The joys and pleasures of step-parenthood must necessarily be closely akin to those which are felt by every 'normal' parent. All parents for instance, are thrilled and proud when their offspring first walk, talk, do well in exams and so on. It is natural. However, when step-parents feel these pleasures there is an extra depth to them for they know that they have had to work hard and make sacrifices in order to feel just like any other parent at these proud moments. To feel just like any other parent has probably been one of your chief aims since marrying and I can vouch for the fact personally, as well as from talking to other step-parents on the subject, that this process can often take years. The first time you spontaneously feel fiercely protective about your step-child is a real breakthrough and a moment to remember. On another occasion you might catch yourself boasting about your step-child's 'special' abilities just like all those other doting parents you used to look down upon but inwardly envied. Sometimes you will look at your step-child laughing or telling a story and feel a great surge of love for no apparent reason which sets you wondering if it's really happening at last. Were those people who always answered 'it comes with time' right after all?

Most parents like to see something of themselves in their children; they like to hear the remark 'he's a chip off the old block, isn't he?' When you as step-parent see a little of yourself in the children, it is a real joy. For months you might be frustrated by the fact that these children are just the opposite of what you would like them to be, then suddenly one day you might catch them quoting one of your favourite opinions or defending certain standards which you have tried to pass on to them but never believed they would adopt. The pleasure this gives is far greater, I feel, than that which a natural parent feels, for you as step-parent have worked so hard, often against the odds, at bringing up the family under no easy circumstances and the rewards, when they come, mean a lot more.

For the step-parent, every family occasion involving happiness, celebration or just plain good fun, has a special deeper meaning. A simple thing such as sitting together in church, or going to a party together, can mean so much after years of struggling to get the family to feel united rather than splintered, made up of 'his', 'hers' and 'ours'. These are occasions which only a step-parent can know and feel, and of which the average ordinary family is hardly aware.

There is real joy to be felt when one day it dawns on you that you have passed a milestone which once you viewed somewhat sceptically, feeling it was out of reach. This milestone appears in various forms. Perhaps it marks the end of a bed-wetting stage for a child who could not adapt to his new circumstances without showing signs of distress. Maybe it marks the beginning of a better relationship between yourself and a child when at last you feel free to talk openly and understand each other. For one step-mother I made friends with, the day her step-daughter spontaneously called her 'Mummy' instead of the usual polite 'Auntie Margaret' was a day of deep joy and she recorded it in her diary, considering it a major milestone passed.

Compliments about your family life from strangers who are unaware of your status are particularly rewarding. You realize that they cannot be flattering you and that outwardly you must appear to be a healthy loving family unit. In the same way, compliments from friends and relatives who once doubted your abilities to unify the family are real music to your ears. To hear my step-sons' grandparents remark how nicely they were growing up gave me more pleasure than they could have thought. Even if it were not my influence affecting them, at least I was not impeding family progress!

On the subject of progress, it is good to look back occasionally as well as forward to the next hurdle. Only then do you fully realize just how far you have come already and can allow yourself a pat on the back and a little glow of satisfaction. See how those children have grown in body and in mind in that time, how much more settled they are with you around. Remember how you yourself used to handle situations and how you now deal with similar occasions — you too have progressed in your understanding. But best of all are those moments within the family when it is plainly demonstrated that those strange children have actually grown to love you, unbelievable though it might have seemed at times. Maybe a bunch of flowers is thrust at you by an awkward boy, or perhaps a diffident little girl will climb voluntarily on to your knee. One of my friends gets a particular pleasure when her step-daughter now living on her own rings up home and nearly always wants to speak to her step-mother, not her father, who resigns himself to passing over the phone almost automatically. Similarly, I enjoy receiving letters from my step-son, addressed just to me. Another friend felt overjoyed to be specially introduced to her young step-daughter's friends at a school disco. 'This is Barbara, my step-mother,' she said proudly, having fetched along the friends deliberately to meet her. Barbara knew she had been accepted at that moment. It is also a pleasure, of course, for the natural parent to see and know that his or her second partner has at last been given the love and respect that was hoped for.

The reverse feeling, that of a loving relationship starting within yourself and reaching out toward the child, is the one already mentioned — that sudden, unaccountable rush of affection welling up inside you. You will know then that in the past you have only been pretending and wishing and that the real thing is happening at last. In other words, the skin graft is imperceptibly 'taking'; you and the family are fusing into one, feeling right as well as looking right.

A step-family can gain a great deal of pleasure from what I have elsewhere called the 'extended family'. An only child is often thrilled to have a step-sister or brother arrive on the scene, especially if you have prepared him or her for the event in a positive way. What a joy it is for the step-parents to see 'his' and 'hers' playing and sharing together. One step-mother told me that her daughter looks forward to the regular visits of her step-sister and really adores her for herself, not because there are treats in store on these occasions. An older couple I know still receive real pleasure from watching how their respective sons 'gel' together, all four of them, even now that visits have become more widely spaced out as they grow older and go their own ways.

There are, too, the obvious joys of a 'mutual' baby which often works wonders towards helping bring family relationships closer together, and the less obvious ones of gaining lots of new relatives all round in the form of aunts, uncles and grandparents. The extended family can grow quite large and bring with it a grand variety of different characters, which often enhances family life.

Having a step-family has enriched my life and I hope this can be said for most other step-parents. By setting yourself goals and ideals and by overcoming difficulties, you become a stronger person in yourself, more able to cope with every demand life makes on you, not only the family demands. You gain a deeper awareness of the values of family love since you have had to work to gain that love and have never taken it for granted. Your particular family's happiness will be gained at a price and will therefore mean much more to you than that of the 'biological' family, who probably never really think about it. Each step-child adds a new dimension to your life; there are unexpected twists and turns during their upbringing as you discover new things which drive and motivate them. I am not saying that all these surprises will be nice ones by any means, but they will keep you on your toes as joint manager of the family and never let you slip into complacency.

Lastly, I would mention the sense of fulfilment and achievement gained from helping to bring up someone else's family. A word of warning first, however. If you enter into your step-marriage thinking to yourself how richly rewarding it will be and how fulfilled you will feel, you will soon have to change your attitude Your hopes will be dashed within weeks if you embark on your new life in that frame of mind — step-parenthood is not for martyrs. The sense of fulfilment I refer to creeps up on you very slowly and gradually, and only after you have suffered many failures and set-backs. When you first feel that sense of having done your best in the circumstances given, you will know also the answer to the question 'Is it all worth while?'

9.

HAVE I GOT WHAT IT TAKES?

When you read through the previous chapters you might get the impression that you have to be super-human to carry through your task successfully. If you hope to achieve your goal immediately, I would agree with you — but you won't, it's not possible. Nevertheless, you will find that you grow in understanding and strength of character, however great your shortcomings at the beginning. You gain impetus as your family situation progresses, and I assure you it will if you have got all the basics right. It will take time and this is what you must remember during all the bad times, Rome wasn't built in a day. I'm going to run through a few of the qualities you will need — they are all of equal importance, until we reach the last one, which you will find is the greatest of them all.

Courage: You have already shown your courage in your readiness to take a big step in the dark. You wouldn't be in the situation that you are in now, if you hadn't already weighed things up and decided to go ahead with what must surely be the biggest step you will take in your life.

Patience: It won't all work out at once as we all secretly hope the day we get married. Step-parenting is a long term process and you must have the patience to 'sit it out'. Always have your sights set well ahead so that you have a goal to aim for — it's a marvellous feeling when you pass one of your milestones!

Determination: You'll need bags of this one! I'm a firm believer in the fact that you can do anything if you are determined enough and believe in it whole-heartedly. It's easy to give up on a few of the principles you started with, but a bit of extra determination will see you through; stick to them, they will be worth it in the end, risk the unpopularity.

Firmness: Closely connected with determination, of course. When you make a decision, act on it. Make your own 'rules', as mentioned earlier. Children like to know where they stand even if they're not keen to accept some of your ideas. I'm sure they respond much better to a firm yes or no, rather than to 'maybe,' 'we'll see,' or 'I don't know.'

Frankness and honesty: These qualities have been fully discussed elsewhere — you must be ready to talk, to discuss matters openly and honestly with your partner and your children if they are old enough. This is probably a stumbling block in many a step-marriage. The step-parent tries so hard to cope with the family situation, to do everything right and to please their partner at the same time, in the way that all newly-married couples try to please. Just because it is second-time round for one or even both of you doesn't alter the fact that you need time to adjust to each other. You probably don't like to complain of anything in case your partner thinks you are unhappy or unable to cope. Bottled up in this way, small issues become really magnified until they get out of all proportion. This sort of attitude will hinder your ability to cope, whereas if you discuss your problem openly as soon as it first appears you can save a whole lot of unnecessary scenes and hurt feelings. How often do you hear friends say 'Well, we never really talked about it,' and you, as the outsider, can see so clearly that if only they had, they would now be getting along much better.

Communication, then, seems to be a most important factor. Whenever possible, the children ought to be brought into discussions too — they are not objects, burdens which you have to bear because you married their parent — their comments and suggestions ought to be given a fair hearing. After all, they are at the base of nearly every discussion you will have concerning your step-marriage.

So swallow your pride, pluck up courage and bring yourself to face facts and discuss them together as a family until you can build up something useful from them again. The more open you are the better chance you will have of succeeding in your step-marriage.

Strength of character: This one may sound very similar to firmness but I make one distinguishing point. I could refer to it as 'thickness of skin' or the ability to withstand adverse criticism. You will sometimes get the blame for behaviour of children or various events which have no bearing on your influence whatsoever. This will seem most unfair, as indeed it is, but you have got to learn to ignore this kind of criticism. It is founded on ignorance; people who have no understanding of your situation whatsoever will always be ready to comment. 'He's only their step-father, he only cares for her really, not for the poor kids,' or 'Oh, they weren't at all like that before she came along,' — these are the kind of hurtful comments you might hear behind your back. My advice is to ignore them; things not said to your face are never worth listening to anyway. If you think there might be a grain of truth attached to criticism, get to work on altering things straight away, be honest with yourself and admit you might perhaps have given cause for criticism, nobody's perfect.

The ability to act: No, we are not adding drama to an already dramatic situation. What I refer to can be illustrated as follows: your step-children put you in a difficult situation perhaps, you have no idea what you ought to do or say. This is the occasion when you have to act; act confidently, and calmly, never display to the children that you are afraid you can't manage them. They will *want* to rely on you as well as their natural parent. They have probably been through a period of doubt and insecurity if there has been separation and divorce and what they need now is confidence that all will be well. Show this confidence in your character, even though it might be wavering privately, then when you have successfully covered up your own doubts and uncertainties, discuss it all later with your partner so that next time a similar situation occurs, you won't need to act.

Common sense: This one will take you a long way. Don't panic, think things out, remember how many thousands of other step-parents just like you exist all over the world. Get it all into proportion this way, for it's quite true, you are just one of many, all facing very similar problems. If there's something you think you can't do, like catering for five when you've never even boiled an egg before, use your common sense, buy a basic book about it, ask those who are happy to advise you without being condescending about it. In other words, do something practical, don't give in to that feeling of failure.

Adaptability and flexibility: Since you are really taking on an unknown quantity in someone else's children it's no good entering your marriage with ready-made, pre-conceived ideas about how you will go about things. About basics, you ought to have your principles sorted out, but you won't know exactly how the children will react to your ideas until it happens, then the fun starts. You've got to be ready for anything, surprised at nothing (at least don't show your surprise!). Adapt to every different situation and be ready to change some of your plans if things don't run in the direction you expected.

Love: We come now to the one quality from which all the others spring, though don't run away with the idea that this is all you need. You could love your step-child to distraction, but without firmness and common sense from you, he would grow up all wrong, wouldn't he? All the other factors have to combine with love. From love springs kindness, consideration for others, self-sacrifice, toleration — in fact all the things we have talked about in previous chapters. Give and take, one of the supreme necessities in your step-marriage (and of course in any relationship) only comes with love, love for your husband or wife, love for their children. The ability to share equally between partner and children, understanding, willingness to sit and listen to the other side of the story, availability and accessibility in times of others' stress — these things and many more all stem from love.

Don't despair if you don't feel an instant parental love for your step-children, it can grow as you and your partner work together through the love which exists for the two of you. Children have a need to be loved and, eventually, when all of you have had time to adjust and get to know each other inside as well as outside you might find that love has grown without your even noticing it. However, never think you have failed if this love does not appear at all on either side. Many step-children to whom I have spoken commented that they were happy just to see their parent happy even though the choice of partner was not their ideal, and said they would settle for friendship rather than parental love. They often thought that friendship was a working possiblity whereas 'parenthood' was out of the question, so please bear this in mind — it might help you to find the best alternative when parental love eludes you.

This chapter is not intended to frighten you off becoming a stepparent although I can already hear the cries of 'Who's going to possess all those qualities?' It is obvious that none of us is going to have all those abilities all at once, but so long as you have a never-ending supply of the greatest of them, love, and can muster up a few of the others when needed you are well on your way to success.

10.

HELP!

Don't worry if you have turned to this section before reading any of the other chapters. You will not be the only one to do so I assure you, for if you have found yourself unable to cope with all the glib-sounding advice and careful point by point planning this is naturally the best chapter to begin with. You may feel in need of a good shoulder to cry on and a patient listener to hear out your problems. Rest assured, there will not be many step-parents who do not come to this pitch at some stage in their career and in my opinion it is definitely a sign of strength, not weakness, to ask for help.

It shows that you have tried to make a go of things, or to plan things out, and are brave and honest enough to admit that you don't think you can manage on your own. If you are asking for help, then it also shows that you still want to try to succeed in spite of either failures or weaknesses. You are half-way to success if you have come to this point, for your determination and your honesty speak for themselves — they are high up on the list of qualities a step-parent needs. You also have the greatest quality of all, love, otherwise you would have abandoned ship without a further thought, wouldn't you? In the majority of cases, you are not alone either in facing your troubles because you have your partner, unless, of course, things have really gone wrong for you both.

Obviously there is not going to be an immediate solution offered to you as if by magic. There are times when human relationships get so entangled, however, that when you are in the middle of them you can't clearly see just what is happening and there seems no way out. This is where a third person can be so helpful if you find the right one. This person can listen to your story without interrupting, exploding into violence, bursting into tears or whatever other reaction might have been involved when you tried talking things over with your partner or your children. You might even feel more at ease when unburdening yourself to a stranger, for you won't be frightened of hurting their feelings or causing anger or bitterness. How often have you found yourself talking to a complete stranger on a bus or train and telling them all manner of private things which have been on your mind but which you previously found impossible to face up to and put into words? You know you won't meet them again, or at least there will be no repercussions on your private life, because they don't know you, have not already judged you, and will not tell any of your friends or relatives about you. Talking to a professional helper such as someone from the Marriage Guidance Council is just like this. They are trained for their job, they are not just nosy people revelling in gossip of a personal nature. They volunteer to fill this position of listener, sympathizer and helper. They know of other people who are also qualified to help you if there is need. You can speak confidently to them, they all have a ready understanding and, if truth were told, have probably heard your problem ten times over in the past week or two.

The Marriage Guidance Council offers an excellent service. You can find their number in the local telephone directory. You become important to them as soon as your first interview is arranged. If you and your partner want to go together for a talk, that's fine, but if you both wish to go separately this is also possible. The person advising you can then get a good idea of the story from both angles. If you go on your own you will not be inhibited by your partner's presence. Going together, however, also has its advantages; you will feel you are fighting the problem together in the hope of finding a solution together.

If you are worried about being 'odd' or 'different' in some way the counsellor will soon put you right on that score. They are very busy people indeed; there is a great need for them in these days of disintegrating marriages, stresses and violence. You will be only one or two of thousands all over Britain who seek help and guidance daily — the very facts and figures concerning remarriages are startling — yet the Marriage Guidance people will never treat you as a number. You become their personal care, they will be available to you whenever possible, just a phone call away.

There are, of course, other bodies or groups of people who are ready to listen and offer help. A minister is not always the pious narrow-minded character you might have thought; he is an ever-ready listener and ought to be able to offer comfort to you in your distress and perhaps calm your mind sufficiently for you to think clearly and constructively about your next move. Anything you tell him will be in absolute confidence, rest assured.

In 1983 the National Stepfamily Association was formed at a conference I was lucky enough to attend in London. The aim of the Association is to bring to the State's notice the need for support and guidance for step-families, to provide a central organization through whom the professional services can seek advice and to promote local active self-help groups, several of which have already been established, with many more in the pipeline.

These local groups hold meetings where you can meet other people in your situation and feel that warmth which comes from knowing that you are not alone against 'the others' who have a normal happy family life. The Association can also put you in touch with a local person who will listen to your problems and give whatever support they can. If you feel self-conscious about approaching a group or an individual face to face they will give you a phone number to ring and you can speak to a sympathetic listener who has volunteered to put his or her experience at your disposal. See the section on further reading for the address and phone number of the Association's headquarters if there is no branch in your area. Have you thought, incidentally, that your own experiences so far could be helpful to others? Local branches need step-parents to be involved and you could well put the handling of your own problems to good use! Think it over — this is how many of the groups begin, and it would mean that you would be doing the community a service by sharing your story.

Many towns have Family Centres — your local Social Services will tell you about them, or simply find them in the directory under Social Services. Gingerbread is a nationwide group which caters for one-parent families and offers constructive help. Your local library will be able to give you many of the names or addresses you might find helpful. The Samaritans, of course, are an ever-present help for those in despair; their number is also in the book. But this is looking very much on the dark side isn't it?

Try to think constructively of all the reasons why you must get help and begin afresh on your step-marriage. The children involved must surely be your first priority. They did not ask to be involved, it is not chiefly their behaviour or misdoings which have caused you to be in the position you are; your own failures must have contributed, and you as adults have to take the initiative in putting things right. If you decide after taking advice that you are never going to cope with your step-children, then you must make the big decision as to whether it might be best for you as step-parent to withdraw from the situation.

However, these are pessimistic thoughts and life is rarely as bad as it seems at the time — we all look back on our bad moments and think how much better we could have handled them, or how stupid we were to let things get out of all proportion. I suggest that after reading through this chapter, you go through the whole guide from the beginning, try to encourage your partner to do the same, then *talk*. Make yourselves analyse your own position, for each one of us has his own particular version of step-parenting, and by discussing in a friendly constructive way, I'm sure many of you will not find the need to ask for help. You will find it within yourselves and feel all the more fulfilled for having faced it together or as a family and will come out at the other side full of hope and ready to build towards a better future.

CONCLUSION

After talking to and reading about many step-parents and their children I cannot be unaware of the fact that even in the cases where the whole operation turned out badly or miserably, where there was opposition, selfishness, lack of discipline, etc., the children involved have gone on to be mature, well-balanced adults on the whole. I cannot find any statistics which prove that step-children are more likely to become criminals, drug-takers, perverts, etc. than any other group of children. Many step-children have spoken to me of their stormy backgrounds with perfect calmness, self-assurance and, with hindsight, understanding for those whom they say made their lives difficult. They are perfectly normal folk and have produced perfectly normal families themselves. Do we not often notice that children brought up under poor circumstances (for example: poor housing, too many in the family, father in prison) can often turn out to have far greater strength of character than the pampered over-indulged children of rich, easy-living parents?

It has been suggested to me that anxious step-parents can become over-sensitive about their position of responsibility, can be too aware of the difference between themselves and normal parents. In other words, they may try too hard and cause things to work against their wishes, even with the best of intentions. Perhaps children are not always as deeply emotionally involved as we imagine. They live for the present usually, and if their tummies are filled, their beds warm and there are others in the family for company who seem to get along OK together, why should they worry about anything deeper?

This is food for thought, isn't it? Remember the skin graft in the introduction to this guide. Sometimes the place treated with the graft will always bear a slight trace or mark, a certain difference in texture, to the rest of the skin. Does this detract from a person's character and nature? Of course not, though they are probably very acutely aware of it if it shows in public. If you are satisfied that you have done all you can to make your 'grafted' family work and become 'normal' you must not then worry if there are still traces of 'differences' about it. There cannot be many perfect families around in any case and if there were, they would be pretty boring ones I am sure, with little to talk about, aim for, or squabble over.

Relax when you feel your major effort is over, reap the rewards and feel glad that you accepted a challenge and did your best under the circumstances given. I can assure you from my own experience that time will be on your side. With time, your stepchildren grow older, wiser; they learn to cope with situations they couldn't handle at a younger age; they alter in character sometimes, perhaps under your influence even. They eventually become independent and go on to lead lives of their own away from home and then many of your awkward differences will be resolved. As adults the relationships take on a different footing and the old resentments and jealousies melt away into the past.

Therefore, all of you who feel you can never achieve the ultimate in step-parenting, take heart; in a few years' time you will look back and be amazed at what you have already achieved, things which at the time seemed impossible. Life is full of surprises and certainly your role as a step-parent will never be boring or dreary. Look to the future with confidence and be ready for anything.

FURTHER INFORMATION

Further Reading
1. *Saturday Parent* by Peter Rowlands (Unwin Paperbacks 1981). This book deals with the subject of access. It discusses in a readable, down to earth manner how the 'access' parent can make the very best of his/her relationship with the children concerned. It also demonstrates to the custodial parents how much they can contribute to the efficiency and all round beneficial effects of the access arrangement.
2. *The Step-parents' Handbook* by Elizabeth Hodder (Sphere, 1985). Chapter 8 on questions of money offers detailed practical advice and Chapter 9 on legal rights and duties is also full of sound facts and figures.

Points of Contact
I list below the four basic organizations which will in turn direct you to more specific contacts where necessary:

1. Citizens Advice Bureau
The number of your local branch will be in the phone book. Here you can present your problem to an understanding and friendly person who will have all the phone numbers and personal contacts for the more specialized organizations.

2. Social Services
The phone book will give you the number and from there you

can find out what your local area has to offer in the way of family or community support. Most towns have a wide range of both statutory and voluntary bodies offering help of a specific nature to families.

3. Marriage Guidance Council
Their number is in the phone book and their services have been mentioned in Chapter 10.

4. Stepfamily, The National Stepfamily Association,
   Room 3
   Ross Street Community Centre
   Ross Street
   Cambridge CB1 3BS

Stepfamily was founded in 1983, its aim being to provide practical support to stepfamilies and promote a better awareness and understanding of step-family problems among the general public and existing statutory bodies concerned with family welfare. Services are as follows:

a) Provides a quarterly newsletter to members.
b) Puts step-parents in touch with one another.
c) Offers a confidential telephone counselling service.
d) Helps set up local Stepfamily support groups.
e) Sends out an up to date book list.
f) Publishes practical informative leaflets dealing with key problem areas.

INDEX

absent parent, 53, 57, 67–70
access, 65-70
  planning for, 34–5
achievement, 93
acquaintanceship period, 14–21
adaptability, 32, 98
age gap, 56
'alien' feelings, 59, 70–3
authority, 12–13, 56–7, 66

babies
  as half-brothers/sisters, 54–5
  as step-children, 18–19
  planning for new, 37
betrayal, feelings of, 53
bribery, 15, 67

case histories, 25, 42, 49, 62, 73, 80, 87
character, of a step-parent, 95–9
church
  ministers, 103
  policy *re* divorce, 41
common interests, 14, 86
common sense, 97–8
communication, 23, 85, 96
comparisons, 30, 48
competition, for affection, 56
compromise, 12, 61
consideration
  for children's feelings, 21–2, 33
  for others, 62, 86
continuity, 35, 47, 68–9
courage, 95
criticism, 77–80, 97
custodial parent, 65–6

death, and grief, 47–8
determination, 73, 96
discrimination, 55, 60–2
discussion, 12–13, 22–3, 85, 96
divided loyalties, 53–62, 69
divorce
  and grief, 47–9
  and weddings, 41
'double' step-family, 20–3, 55, 60–2

enjoyment, of family time, 84–7
enrichment of life, 92
'ex-parent', 67–70
extended family, 79, 92

family
  extended, 79, 92
  starting a new, 37, 54–5
  togetherness, 83–7
Family Centres, 103
favouritism, 55, 60–2
finances, 32, 35–6, 84
frankness, 17, 22–3, 96
fresh start, 29–33
  pros, 30–1
  cons, 32–3
fulfilment, 93

generation gap, 79–80
Gingerbread, 104
gossip, 78
grandparents, 45–6, 79–80
grief, 47–9
guilt, 32–3, 57, 59, 67

half-brothers/sisters, 54–5
home
    a new, 29–33
    another person's, 72–3
honeymoon, 42

indoctrination, 46
insecurity
    after disruptions, 34, 47, 55
    financial, 32
integration of two families
    after marriage, 60–2
    during acquaintanceship
        period, 20–3
interference
    from absent parent, 30, 57,
        65–7
    from relatives, 30, 77–80
interim period, 45–49

jealousy, 53–62
joys of step-parenting, 89–93

loss and grief, 47–9
love
    from a step-child, 91
    parental, 87, 90, 98–9
loyalties and jealousies, 53–62

maintenance payment, 35–6,
    57–8
marriage,
    ceremony, 40–2
    telling the children, 16–19
Marriage Guidance Council, 25,
    102, 108

names, 37–40

one-parent family, 46–7, 59, 71
over-sensitivity, 10, 21–2, 105

past
    children's, 45–49
    reminders of the, 31, 65, 72
patience, 19, 47, 95

planning
    practicalities, 29–43
    preliminaries, 11–27
pleasure
    from a step-family, 89–93
privacy, 13, 61
progress, 91
public opinion, 33, 41, 80
punishment, 13

rejection, 54, 58–9
relatives, 77–8
    and the interim period, 45–6
    early interference from, 30
    grandparents, 79
remarriage
    introducing the idea, 16–19
    the ceremony, 40–2
respect, 56–7, 61, 73
responsibilities, 12, 46–7, 60–1,
    84, 86
rewards, of step-parenting,
    89–93
rules and regulations, 12–13,
    86, 96

schools, 13, 32, 78
security
    continuity and, 35, 47
    financial, 32
self-help groups, 49, 103
sharing
    interests, 14, 86
    problems, 23, 49, 103
Social Services, 107
standards, different sets of,
    12–13, 22, 69
Stepfamily Association, 103, 108
step-syndrome, 37–8
surnames, 40
'sweeping clean', 70–2
sympathy, 21–2, 47–9

'takeover' of family, 45–9
team spirit, 85–6
tension, 69–70

time
- for the family, 14, 19–20, 84, 86
- organization of, 59, 83–4
- to adjust, 47
- to think, 23–5
- to yourselves, 24, 59

togetherness, 83–87

united front, 12–13
unity, of family, 55, 60–2, 70–1, 83–7
upbringing, principles of, 12–3

wedding, 40–2
'wicked' step-parent, 15, 77, 80
working wives, 36, 84

Other titles of interest to parents:

Let's Cook It Together
Utterly Scrumptious Recipes for Adults and Children — Vegetarian Style
PEGGY BRUSSEAU

There are vegetarian cookbooks for adults, and there are vegetarian cookbooks for children — but this is the first 'do-it-together' vegetarian cookbook. All the recipes are easy to make and use healthy and delicious ingredients. Clear step-by-step instructions divide tasks between parent and child, with symbols to show just who does what. Exciting recipe names like 'Stars in a Blizzard', 'Jump and Shout' and 'Fruity Goop' are guaranteed to coax any child into the kitchen, and parents will be delighted to know that they taste as good as they sound!

Will You Read Me a Story?
The Parent's Guide to Children's Books
TONY BRADMAN

Here is a guide for every new parent who has ever felt overwhelmed by the wealth of wonderful children's books on the market today. As well as recommendations of books for babies, toddlers, pre-school children and beyond, there is sound practical advice on making books a really enjoyable part of family life from the earliest days. Tony Bradman is Deputy Editor of *Parents* magazine, founder of the 'Best Books for Babies' Award, and the father of three young children.